JAMES WELLS

OF

MONTANA

James Wells
c. 1875
Fort Benton, Montana

JAMES WELLS

OF

MONTANA

The Years 1860–1885

JAMES A. FRANKS

WILD GOOSE PRESS
Santa Cruz, California

A percentage of the royalties from this book will go to the
Fort Belknap Reservation in Montana.

The cover photograph was taken by the author at the
Judith Landing National Historic District in Montana. The
stone building was built by James Wells in 1882 as a
warehouse for freight coming up the Missouri River and is
considered one of Montana's most historic buildings.

A mong all the frontiersmen I have known, the one that more than any other realized my conception of an ideal was James Wells...

— Henry MacDonald
"A Pioneer"

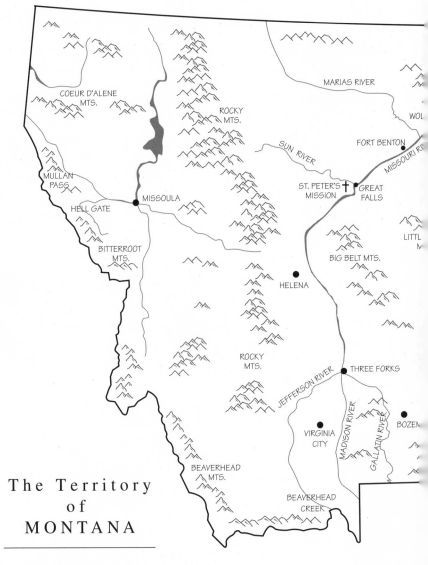

COEUR D'ALENE MTS.

MARIAS RIVER

ROCKY MTS.

WOL

SUN RIVER

FORT BENTON

MISSOURI RI

MULLAN PASS

ST. PETER'S MISSION

GREAT FALLS

HELL GATE

MISSOULA

BITTERROOT MTS.

BIG BELT MTS.

LITTL M

HELENA

ROCKY MTS.

THREE FORKS

JEFFERSON RIVER

MADISON RIVER

GALLATIN RIVER

BOZEM

VIRGINIA CITY

BEAVERHEAD MTS.

BEAVERHEAD CREEK

The Territory
of
MONTANA

N

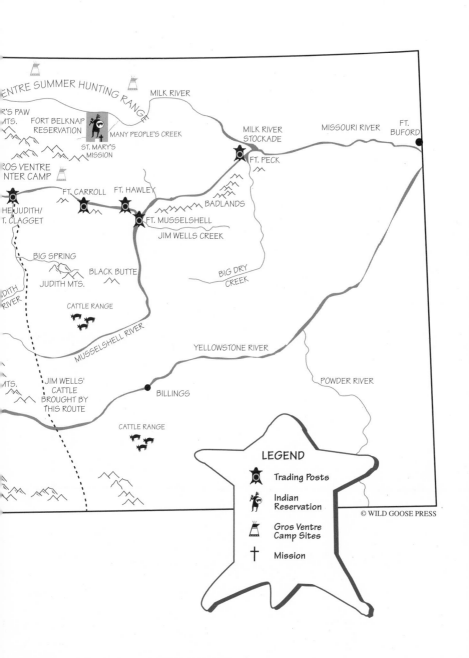

CONTENTS

PREFACE

*J*AMES WELLS OF MONTANA is a story that took me more than seven years to track down and tell.

Over the years I had collected many anecdotes about my family history, but if I needled my mother for further detail, her reply was often: I can't be sure, or, I don't remember. Still, she had been very close to her own mother, and the stories she did recall were clear and vivid. One thing I learned early on was that my great-grandfather, James Wells, had gone to the Montana Territory from Indiana by way of California, around 1865. That he had once gotten so sick out on the range that he had been nursed to health by a tribe of Gros Ventre Indians was already legendary in our family.

I began to take trips to Montana and started my research on James Wells at the River Press in Fort Benton with Joel Overholser. He had just finished his book, *Fort Benton: World's Innermost Port,* and he showed me numerous clippings naming James Wells, as well as A. J. Noyes' *In the Land of Chinook,* which also mentions Wells as one of the first fifteen whites living in the Montana Territory.

One thing led to another. The clippings prompted me to go to the Historical Society in Helena and sort through the records of the U.S. Senator, T.C. Power. There I discovered a number of transactions between Power and Wells including records of their partnerships. And it was there that I learned that James Wells had married a Gros Ventre Indian who had the Christian name of Maggie, the name I knew as belonging to my great-grandmother. I was delighted yet amazed that this had not been among the many other things I had learned about my Montana history. Now I was beginning to see the true shape of Wells' life and had two trails to follow.

To research Maggie Wells I made many trips to the Gros Ventre reservation at Fort Belknap. There I was able to interview a number of the older members of the tribe to verify some of the traditions and living conditions of the Gros Ventres. I also learned I could go to Washington D.C. to the National Archives and pull records pertaining to when Maggie lived on the reservation, which I did. And in the next few years, as I became consumed by this project, I poured through numerous works on the history of Montana and its native peoples, all of which were invaluable sources adding to the richness of my story.

As for my method of composing *James Wells of Montana*, I have taken obvious liberties with dialogue, but the names of all places and the events reported in the life of James Wells are authentic, as are the names of the principal characters.

But perhaps of the greatest surprise to me in undertaking this project was discovering that my own mother, Marguerite Hildegarde Franks, was registered on the reservation as a Gros Ventre. Never had she told us, as this affiliation had been a source of great discomfort to her mother, Mary Wells, growing up at the turn of the century when everything she had, including her mother Maggie, had been stripped away from her without apology because of her Indian blood. It was a profound revelation to uncover this avenue into my family's past. After pulling together a life's accumulation of events, the story of James Wells became more than my family history; *James Wells* is the story of the mixing of cultures and of the many pioneer families of Montana.

Acknowledgments

I must start with my oldest daughter, Annemary Franks, M.D., who took the first trip to Montana with me and started me on my research.

My wife Marianne, my sons James and Joseph and my daughters Elizabeth and Emily have all been enormously patient and supportive.

I am very grateful to Catherine Halver and Truby Stiffarm at the Fort Belknap Reservation in Montana and to the Montana Historical Society for their cooperation and help.

And finally to Elizabeth McKenzie, who kept me on track during the whole process of finishing this book.

JAMES WELLS

OF

MONTANA

CHAPTER ONE

The New West

J AMES WELLS STOOD on the deck of the Pacific Mail Steamship
as it entered the harbor at San Francisco. It was February of
1860 and Jim was twenty-five; he was a slender young man with
auburn hair and the beginning of a moustache. He could see his
brother John standing on the bow of the ship, eager to touch
ground as they completed the long journey. Their father had
given them the passage money to travel from the family farm
in Indiana to New York, from where they had sailed down to
Panama and crossed the Isthmus. The sweltering heat of the
overland crossing through Panama had made the rest of the
ocean trip seem easy. At last they were finally there.

Jim's father had been generous in allowing them the best on
their journey west but they had tried not to advertise it. Jim
looked around the ship and saw those who had sold everything
to get to California, many near starvation — he had heard
stories on the boat about passengers getting their throats cut for
as little as a dollar.

Jim knew it had been hard on their father, seeing his two sons leave home, yet he had himself known what it was like to seek adventure.

The son of a cotton farmer, James Wells Sr. left North Carolina when he was twenty years old. He had been given the opportunity to move to Indiana to purchase a 600-acre farm and a small trading post on the Cumberland Road in Indiana. It promised to be an excellent move, since it was along the Cumberland that most all wagons heading west traveled.

Jim's father arrived in Indiana in 1832. He met Mary a year later. She was a young school teacher who had been raised in the Indiana Territory. They were soon married and their first son was James William Wells, born in the spring of 1835, named after his father and his grandfather. John Wells was born a year later.

Raised on the fringe of the West, the boys learned to ride and shoot from the time their father could put them on a horse. But the strong hand of their mother also guided them. They were schooled and learned how to run a store. The Cumberland brought the wagons right by the trading post, many stopping for last supplies before St. Louis. The family could feel the high level of anxiety among the travellers, since this was only the beginning of the long journey west; as a boy, Jim couldn't help wondering what would become of them.

"You think this trip's been bad," the Captain of the steamship told Jim. "You might have tried overland. Back in forty-nine, this very ship made her maiden voyage. She left New York before the excitement began, and by the time she rounded the Cape and steamed into Panama, near fifteen hundred people were pushing and shoving to board for San Francisco. Only four hundred could go. Fare was up to one thousand dollars each."

"We know it," Jim replied. "Our store was never empty that year."

"Why weren't you boys out here for the rush?"

"Gold and silver can fail. Dad always told us: 'Soil may erode or decline, but it's always capable of rebuilding.' We want land."

"Tell that to the thousands of folks that've poured out here since forty-nine. Some've made it rich, but by far the rest of 'em are scrambling for flecks. Then they go and spend it one weekend in town. That's not for me either. You boys look serious. I think you'll do well out here."

The captain went on to tell Jim that although many of the passengers of the ships would rush off to the mines, many were smart enough to stay in the city and establish themselves in business. Miners would always need supplies. San Francisco suddenly had a population of around 50,000; other cities like Sacramento, San Jose and Stockton were growing too, largely to help supply the numerous mining camps with food and equipment.

"Why don't you boys stay on the ship for a couple days until you get your bearings? Here's the *San Francisco Bulletin*. Word's out that good men are being hired in Sacramento to ride for the Pony Express. Take a look." Jim took the paper and read through it with interest. Russell, Majors and Waddell had decided to start a Pony Express between St. Joseph, Missouri and Placerville, California, starting the third of April. The cost for through letter service would be five dollars in gold for every half ounce, with rates for shorter distances prorated. Post riders were to be given from $100 to $150, with extra pay for longer runs. It sounded promising.

The brothers spent a few days wandering around the scruffy city of San Francisco; they returned at night to sleep on the boat, which was being cleaned and stocked for its return voyage. One night they got to talking with one of the freight handlers on the dock. His name was Bonnar and he had arrived from Scotland three years before. "What do you think of it out here?" Jim asked him.

"Not so bad," Bonnar replied. "But too many people. Next year I'm on my way up to the Montana Territory. All open land up there, very few whites and many Indians. The buffalo grass grows a foot or two high, as far as you can see. To see it is something."

From his early years at his family's store, Jim had learned to listen to people; he wondered if he would ever get up into the vast, wild areas of the country he had heard so much about. He imagined he would.

Within another day Jim found out that some of the best horses were being raised in San Jose, so he and John headed down to outfit themselves. In San Jose they picked up two good riding horses, and a pair of the specially designed saddles coming out of St. Louis: one third the weight of saddles normally used in the West, with a lot more thought for comfort. By March 18, Jim and John checked in at the St. George Hotel in Sacramento, proving themselves to be two of the first riders equipped and ready for work.

The riders couldn't weigh over 135 pounds. Jim weighed in at 132, while John went over the limit at 140 and had to come back a few days later, slimmed down on a quick diet of coffee and cabbage. They were hired. They received their mail sacks, or *mochilas*, to throw over their horses. These *mochilas* had four locked pockets of hard leather sewn to the blanket and were lined with oilskin to protect the mail from horse sweat, rain, snow and river water when the rider had to swim across. The *mochila* could hold no more than twenty pounds.

The distance Jim was expected to cover ranged from thirty-five to seventy-five miles, depending on the terrain. His speed was to average nine miles per hour. Every twelve or fifteen miles on his run, stations were being constructed; at each station the rider was told to allow no more than two minutes to transfer his cargo to a fresh mount. Jim would ride three horses to make up his ride.

Jim Wells' route was from Carson City and Camp Floyd. It was a lonely stretch on a raw new trail, but it saved more than one hundred miles.

Jim quickly took note of which relay stations were his favorites to stop at. Some were nearly little villages now, where he could spend the night in a room and have a good meal, and even have his horse shoed by a blacksmith if necessary. And it was always a relief to ride in and find a station functioning; many were raided, and more station keepers were murdered than were riders. Paiutes were generally thought to be the guilty parties. Jim himself was wounded late that summer when he was spotted by a group of Paiutes up on a ridge. He received a swift, sharp arrow through his left shoulder, and felt that his life was only saved by his fast, grain-fed horse.

In the late fall and after only nine months of work with the Pony Express, James Wells headed back for San Francisco to find another job. His brother John followed suit. The Wells Fargo office was hiring and was looking for good drivers with their type of experience. The company now covered the whole of the Pacific Northwest.

The man to see was James Birch. Birch had come to California in 1849 from New England where he had been a stage driver. He began his stage line in 1849, using an old wagon drawn by four Mexican broncos. Travel by stage coach between all major areas in California was now said to be as good, if not better, than in any other state.

When John and Jim walked into Wells Fargo they were asked four questions: whether they could drive a stage, whether they could drive like hell, if they liked to work, and if they drank whisky. They answered yes to all but the last question.

The routes reached from San Francisco, south to San Jose, Gilroy, Monterey, Santa Cruz, San Miguel, San Luis Obispo, and occasionally to Los Angeles; east to Fresno, Visalia, Mariposa, Sonora and Columbia. North to Sacramento; from Sacramento to Placerville, Coloma, Nevada City, Yreka, Eureka and all stops in between.

Driving was an education for Jim. The days were long — he covered fifty or sixty miles in a day, resting overnight to return the next. But he was paid well, up to one hundred dollars a month, which included food and room while on the highways.

As the months went by, Jim got to know many of the other drivers, but the one who made the biggest impression was named Charlie Parkhurst. Charlie drove all the long routes, in addition to being an expert woodchopper and keeping up a small farm. Charlie also seemed to look a great deal like a woman and to have a strangely high voice, but of course, a woman would never be allowed a job driving a stage. Charlie was one of the best drivers, and neither Jim nor any of the other drivers wanted to spill "his" secret.

Jim enjoyed the respect he received as a stage driver. Everyone fought to sit up on the box with him. He learned to be clever organizing passengers and luggage. He dressed well and passengers were generous with tips. They even offered hats, gloves, boots, pies and cakes, or a good cigar.

It wasn't a bad life, but after a few years Jim began to focus on the idea of land again — and California was already too crowded for him. The Montana Territory stirred in his imagination. The Civil War was finally over, President

Lincoln had just been assassinated; word was out that the thousands of discharged soldiers from both sides of the long battle would be spreading out all over the country looking for new opportunities and new lives. Jim felt this was the time to go.

Jim and John quit their jobs the last week of April, 1865. They headed for Sacramento, spent two weeks gathering the wagon and supplies, and hit the trail to Montana by early May. After buying a wagon, horses and supplies, they would still have about $4,000 when they made it to Fort Benton, and by selling supplies they might each have another $1,000 back.

They made it to Carson City by the second week in May; now the long trip from Carson City to Salt Lake City lay ahead of them. This trip took thirty days; the weather stayed cool and they arrived in Salt Lake City the second week in June. North to Fort Hall took nine days, putting them near the end of the month. They were able to sell some of their supplies at a good profit to the Army, whose supplies had been raided by the Blackfeet. From here they headed to Virginia City, which took another ten days. From Virginia City to Helena took another week; it was now the middle of July.

Helena was a real community, although it wasn't as large as Salt Lake City. Its government and law and order were difficult to maintain, but it was a place for a good hot meal and a bath.

Helena was also a place to sell all the supplies and one of the wagons for top dollar. There were a great many Chinese there, the only ones Jim had seen since leaving California. On the second night of a four-day stay, Jim and John were able to see a professional boxing match for fifty cents, which included dinner at a local saloon.

Most of the food was monotonous, the usual being bread,

bacon, beans and coffee, but if they were willing to pay the price they could buy green fruit, eggs, and butter. Fresh meat was always available because the cattle industry was developing quickly, and trout abounded in the rivers and streams.

After four days in Helena, Jim and John were ready to move on to Great Falls. This would take another week, but traveling was easy with only one wagon and team, carrying supplies only for themselves.

Just outside of Great Falls they stopped at St. Mary's Mission, and were impressed by a school, an orphanage, and a well-run farm. The sisters were Ursuline and the priests Jesuit. Jim and John were fed a good meal at the mission. They wanted to pay, but were only allowed to make a small donation.

They arrived in Great Falls; it wasn't much of a community and they wondered why it existed, but it was their first sighting of the great Missouri River. They had followed it from Helena, but its true force showed here at Great Falls.

From Great Falls to Fort Benton was only a day and a half's ride, completed the last week of July.

The Wells brothers had timed it right. This was the peak time for the distribution of supplies that had come upriver during the boating season. Fort Benton was known by some as the toughest, busiest town in the West, since it was as far as boats could come up the Missouri River. About 6,000 tons of supplies came through in 1865. It had been a terrible river year and much trans-ferrying of freight from boat to boat had occurred. About 2,000 tons were left at fur posts down the Missouri.

When they arrived in Fort Benton, Jim smiled and thanked his good luck for everything he had seen and for all the opportunity ahead of him. What had taken Jim and his brother on this long trip from Indiana? Working in California

for the Pony Express and Wells Fargo, now to the wilderness of
the Montana Territory; this was part of the vast white
migration.

CHAPTER TWO

Fort Benton

JIM WELLS AND HIS BROTHER arrived in Fort Benton, Montana on a hot July day in 1865.

Fort Benton was an ugly little camp, but compared to the trading posts Jim had seen it was a city. Houses and businesses stood on one side of the short main street, and the Missouri River flowed past on the other. A few frame buildings were spread among the log cabins, some with real glass windows rather than greasepaper. Like most small settlements, it smelled of horses and hides, and from the numerous saloons came the odor of whiskey, smoke, and people who had not bathed for months. Fort Benton was known as the town of waiting, either for the break-up of the river, for the arrival of the steamboats, or for the freeze that would send the town back into its winter sleep.

July was the height of the steamboat season, and the saloons were filled and rowdy all through the night. Bottles littered the floors and roadway. Jim and John split up that first afternoon for a quick reconnaissance. When they met again at dusk, Jim had good news for John.

"I found out they're forming a caravan of some two hundred fifty wagons to go out to the Milk River to pick up freight left by a steamboat called Yellowstone. Might give us a good look at the country, and maybe we could see where we want to settle. We can have the job if we want it. We pull out in two days. Trip takes about fifteen, with a couple days loading at the Milk River and then the trip back. Pay is thirty dollars each, forty dollars for our wagon and team, plus our food and feed for the team. Sound good?"

"It does," said John. "By the way, where in the hell is the Milk River?"

Jim went on to tell his brother that the river was located to the northeast, that it couldn't be any rougher country than they had already traveled, and that they would be paid upon their return.

"They say in winter here it's so cold your words freeze and drop to the ground and never reach the next person," Jim said. He had gotten into conversation with a couple of men over at the freight office who went wolfing in the winter, and made good money on wolf skins.

"Looks like we'll be sleeping in the wagon along the levee, but at least it's not cold," John said. "And we can find someplace to eat. I sure don't want to cook anymore for awhile."

"I appreciate not having to eat your cooking," said Jim.

"One thing I know already is you can't drink that river," John said. "Looks thick enough to walk on."

"If you can walk on it, I'll buy you dinner."

Jim and John walked down the main street of Fort Benton. They noticed a Chinese laundry, and wondered if there was an opium den in back like they had seen in San Francisco. They also saw some well built barns and corrals and were amazed by the amount of freight stacked up on the levees.

"It seems to me everything that comes into this community is shipped out," Jim said. "I hope we can find a place to eat other than the saloons, and something other than beans. I didn't think those Spaniards got all the way from California to this territory, but their beans sure did."

"This place has its own brewery. I wonder how the stuff tastes and if it's made with this Missouri mud?"

The brothers finally decided on a little restaurant on the main street with curtains and clean tablecloths. They looked at the menu posted on the door: "First choice: beefsteak, beans, bread and coffee. Second choice: buffalo hump or tongue, beans, bread and coffee. Third choice: fish from the river, beans, bread and coffee. All you can eat for fifty cents."

"Well, John, I'm not sure about those last two. I think I'll stick with the beef."

"I'll take the same."

A tall, stocky man seated them when they entered.

"Good evening, gents. I'm Roger Perkins, owner of this restaurant. Not seen you around here before. Passing through or staying?"

They shook hands and introduced themselves. "Just got into Fort Benton," Jim said. "We're going to make that trip to Milk River for freight I think. This isn't a bad community though, from what we've seen so far. Like to stay around."

"Yeah," said John. "We hauled supplies from California and got top dollar in Helena."

"How come you're not going to the gold fields?" asked Perkins.

"Well," said Jim, "I'm not the digging type, and don't figure to be lucky enough to find gold."

Later, after they were served their meal, John said, "Hey Mr. Perkins. This is pretty good food and especially your coffee. I have one question to ask you: you talk about all that freight. What percent of it is beans?"

Perkins laughed and said, "Beans are the food that will make the West, if all that gas doesn't blow it away."

"What's for breakfast?" asked Jim.

Perkins laughed some more. "Beans. Can get you an egg for two bits extra and we do have some bacon, no extra for that."

In the morning the brothers were eager for breakfast, but first they wanted to find a laundry. "Got all those rotten clothes together?"

"Hey John, you know any Chinese? I thought you might have picked up a few words in San Francisco."

"The only thing I learned in San Francisco was, 'No goddamned starch in my clothes.' That first batch I got back stood up in the corner by itself and when I put it on, it cut me everywhere it touched me, but those long johns were the worst. I couldn't button the flap shut," he said.

"I bet all our clothes turn out the color of that river," Jim said. "You see out back, how they boil all that laundry? Probably use the water to make soup."

"Come on, that's terrible. Let's go eat."

They ended up in Perkins' restaurant, hungrier than the night before. Perkins greeted them and served them eggs and bacon and coffee.

"You boys know about all the Indian trouble we're having around here?" Perkins asked them.

"Perkins," said Jim, "how come we came all the way up from Salt Lake and never had any trouble, and we just had two big wagons and our team?"

"Just damned luck," said Perkins. "There's lots of trouble going on around here. Piegans, who used to be friendly to the whites, have now joined the Blackfeet, who've been on the warpath a long time. So right after they burnt the Sun River fort, twelve men from here at Benton decided to go on an Indian hunt. They only went a mile and a half, found three Piegan, not a war party or anything. Took them down by the river, hung them on the cottonwood trees, and left them. When word got out, the Indians started killing whites on sight, and now you can't go to the Teton River three miles away without a big group of men to get your wood or game."

"Geez," said Jim.

Perkins went on to tell them that the Missouri River had been the only route to the Montana mines from the east, and this was why they received such a good price for their goods in Helena. Only eight boats came through to Fort Benton. They worked in groups, moving goods a hundred miles or so upriver, unloading them and going back for more. Most were sheathed in boiler-plate to ward off Indian attacks, logged close to 10,000 miles running shuttle on the upper Missouri, and never even reached Fort Benton. The Deer Lodge brought the freight into Fort Benton while the steamboat Benton served as the middle boat, and the General Grant worked the river below the Benton to St. Louis. The boats had to fight off Indian attacks at all loading places, and from points where the channel ran close to the shore, but at twelve and a half cents to fifteen cents per pound, it was sizeable profit. "That's the way you'll be going tomorrow, to pick up freight that couldn't come upriver by boat when the water dropped too low."

"Say, Mr. Perkins," asked John. "This trip we're taking — you think we'll be attacked?"

"With as many wagons and men you got going, no Sioux would be crazy enough to try and hit you," said Perkins. "But down at a place called Ophir, they were working all spring laying out their town site, building cabins, but then a war party killed some wood choppers, and no more Ophir."

"Well, Perkins, one good thing about eating here. We get good food and learn a lot about this place. We'll be back for dinner; want to wander about Benton before that long trip with the wagon train tomorrow. We pull our number today to see where we'll be in line. Sure hate to be the last wagon," said Jim.

Later that day, Jim felt they ought to check on the wagon and make sure the wheels were greased, and to check the team to make sure all the shoes were on tight and in good shape. "Looks like the freight'll be piled on to the top," Jim said.

That afternoon the brothers went and checked out the Fort itself. Jim found it to be well built — the wall was two and a half feet thick, all of adobe brick. There were six major buildings, plus the two blocks on the corners, twenty feet high. It looked like most of the warehouses and housing were outside the fort. After looking over the town they ended the day having a beer at one of the many saloons.

"Thank you, bartender. Say, this beer is almost cold, even if it does taste like horse piss, which it probably is. How do they keep this stuff cold?" said John.

"They have ice packed in the cellar. They cut it off the river in the winter, pack the wall in the cellar. Ice keeps for months," Jim replied.

"Want another?" John asked.

"Are you joking? That one was bad enough. Will have to try the whiskey next time. Which is probably made from that river," said Jim.

"I'm ready. This saloon's dead and smells that way also," John muttered.

They returned to their favorite restaurant.

"Good evening Perkins. We'll have two of your specials. Beefsteak, that is. When you bring it, could you sit a spell with us?" said Jim.

When he did, Jim asked him about the local fur trade, and Perkins was pleased to share what he knew.

"There are two main fur companies, the American and the Northwest, but the big money is in freight here. Freight rates are seven and eight cents to Helena, with large contracts going for five cents a pound and you get soldiers to guard freight trails free, so you profit on the supplies and sending them."

"Well," said Jim, "We'll get our first taste of being freight haulers tomorrow. We'll see you when we get back."

At dawn they pulled their number: forty-seventh out of two hundred fifty. The caravan started to move and would extend for miles. Almost immediately, dust began to rise in choking clouds. "Just think of the last wagon," Jim said. "We should be on our way back by the time he gets started. Where in the hell did all these wagons come from? Didn't see this many around yesterday. Do you think they've been putting them together all night? How they going to feed all this stock and us freighters?"

"Damn," said John. "I thought I talked a lot and asked questions. But you ain't shut up yet. This damn team's sure spooky today. Guess they don't like all the company, but they'll settle down. Maybe we should spend the winter out getting wolf skins; seems like easier work."

"Those guys I talked to told me a little how it's done," Jim told his brother. "You go out in the beginning of winter when the hides are best, with plenty of ammunition, coffee, salt and strychnine. You live and sleep on the prairie like an animal. You travel in small parties, since too many horses and wagons attract the Indians. You watch out or you might lose your horse to Indians and be stranded on the plains in winter. The Indians don't like the white man out in buffalo country. The strychnine in the bait often kills their dogs; as the Indians travel from camp to camp, dogs are their food. Even the friendly tribes will cut up your furs and take your horses."

"Fine, but how do they get these wolves?"

Jim explained that first the hunters killed and partially skinned several buffalo. These were shot at a distance from each other, so as to attract more wolves. Then each buffalo was cut open and had its quarters severed so it would lie flat. The wolfer mixed a bottle of poison with the blood, made small cuts all over the carcass, and laced the incisions with poison. The scrap meat, liver, lungs and tripe were dipped into the poisoned blood and were left on the carcass. Half an ounce of strychnine was enough for each buffalo. One poisoned buffalo would be enough to wipe out about sixty wolves. When the bait was frozen it went a lot farther, as the wolves could not eat it so fast. But apparently there was little time for the fresh meat to freeze, as the wolves often gathered and sat in a half-circle about a hundred yards off while the wolfer prepared the bait.

On the trip east along the Milk River the teams made about fifteen miles a day, giving time to graze and rest. The cooks did a good job feeding about 300: two meals, breakfast and dinner, with lots of beef, beans and coffee. The men sat around campfires, singing along to banjos and fiddles that were brought by team members. People were tired and bedded down early, but a watch was put out to protect the teams.

The third day out they saw a bunch of Assiniboine Indians hunting buffalo. The group didn't look friendly; they didn't like the wagon train. Jim tried to identify some of the tribes. The Sioux were the most numerous and the ones to watch. He had heard they would steal the stock along with a few scalps. The men at the campfire talked about how much they had lost in the past to the Sioux and Crow.

On the ninth day, where the Milk River and the Lodge River met, they came to their first Gros Ventre encampment of about thirty lodges.

They were in the heart of the area held by the Gros Ventres. It ranged along the Milk River, on the east side of the Missouri, extending as far as the Cypress Mountains. From this line to the Marias River, it was level country, well covered with grass for pasturage of buffalo. It was an ideal area in winter. The tribe camped along the banks of the Milk River where wood for fuel could be obtained; in the summer they followed the buffalo.

Jim had heard good things about this particular tribe. He was told to figure about four people to a lodge, or about one hundred twenty people, with about thirty-five warriors. They camped near them, and Jim, without knowing why he wanted to, quickly volunteered to be one of the eight men who would go into the Gros Ventre camp to do some trading.

Jim was introduced to Horse Capture, the chief of this band of Gros Ventres. Horse Capture spoke English and invited the men to have a smoke with him; the tobacco had a funny taste. Jim was fascinated by the tipis and by the clean and graceful appearance of the camp, in contrast to the ugly mess usually left behind in the camps of the traders. The Gros Ventres had many bands who got together in the summer for the Big Hunts, splitting into smaller groups in winter. This band, Jim was told, had wintered down on the Judith.

The men didn't stay long because they would be on the trail early again in the morning. But Jim did give the chief a couple of extra blankets. Horse Capture was pleased and presented Jim with some dried buffalo meat. It seemed Jim had made a friend.

Jim was told that the Gros Ventres were a very proud people. They had suffered a couple of bouts of smallpox and seemed to be fighting almost all the other tribes, but they had been sticking pretty close to the Blackfeet. They did have some of the best buffalo range.

The teams were out about fourteen days and getting closer to Fort Peck and the Milk River stockade, and were coming into Sioux country.

Sixteen days out they came to Fort Peck. Fort Peck was erected by Durfee and Peck to replace their store at Fort Buford. It was the most important establishment of its kind on the Upper Missouri River between Fort Union and Fort Benton, but it was more crudely constructed than most of the old American Fur Company outposts. It was squeezed along a narrow shelf of bottom land, twelve miles above the mouth of the Milk River and looked as though it had been thrown together in a few hours time. There was almost no room to drive a horse behind the stockade and a wagon could barely pass in front of the post and turn into one of its corrals.

The yellow cliff rising behind the Fort seemed to make the trading post wide open and vulnerable for attack.

Jim and John Wells met the men at Fort Peck: Bill Bent and a huge Canadian half-breed called "Frenchy." They didn't seem to have much to trade: flour, oatmeal, bacon, salt, sugar and coffee, and a few Henry, Spencer and Springfield rifles.

It was a short run from Fort Peck to the Milk River stockade. This stockade was just a couple of cabins surrounded by mountains of freight. It was run by five men: the boss Joe Bushway, John Fattig, who was a giant, middle-aged man with a rugged face and a black beard, John's partner "Yankee" Davis, and the twin brothers Jim and Tim McGinnis.

Jim talked to Jim and Tim after they got the wagon loaded, asking what they did during the long winter months. They told him they worked as wood hawks, or wood cutters, in summer. Cottonwood sold for five or six dollars a cord and cedar from eight to twenty dollars per cord. In winter, they turned to the profitable work of hunting and trapping in the area between the Milk and Missouri Rivers. A good beaver fur brought as high as six dollars; wolves, from a dollar and a half to three dollars. Red fox pelt sold for about two dollars, grey fox and coyote for less. Buffalo robes were worth three to five dollars, and even more for especially fine ones. Muskrat, otter, bear, elk, antelope, and deer prices varied according to the demand and the trading post where they were sold. Buffalo tongues, considered delicacies, brought high prices. The tongues were known to sell for as much as four dollars apiece.

The return trip to Fort Benton was uneventful. The Wells brothers did see vast herds of buffalo, easy to shoot to supply extra meat at the meals. Jim experimented and found that the tongues and humps were indeed the best part of the buffalo. They arrived back at Fort Benton in early September.

By the end of the trip, Jim and John had decided to spend a winter out in the Judith area as hunters and trappers. They would use the next month preparing for this new adventure, and felt they had learned a lot listening to the talk of the trappers.

Wolfing sounded the best since there was no need to shoot and shots could attract Indians. Also, the Judith River area had buffalo, which meant lots of wolves.

The first morning back they headed for breakfast at Perkins'. They figured it would be a couple of days before they got their wagon unloaded. There was even talk of re-packing the wagon and sending it on to the mines, which would be all right and pass the time until their big hunt.

Perkins was glad to see the two brothers, and to hear of their adventure and how they felt about the country.

"Well, Mr. Perkins, we got all the way to the Milk River without any Indian trouble, but Fort Peck isn't in too happy of a state. The Sioux have been moving into their area and aren't too friendly. Guess they've killed a few more woodcutters and pushed people back into the forts for protection — if you want to call that place protection. Poorly built, with a cliff rising over it which you could spit into the fort from. Guess the Sioux are big trouble."

"Not just the Sioux," said Perkins. "You know, we keep giving the Indians land and taking it back as we find gold or whatever else. Somehow it just don't make sense. But here I am making my living out here feeding the people coming through."

"What do you think about John and me trapping for a season out in the Judith area? Seems like buffalo and wolf skins are bringing in a good dollar; it would be a good adventure for a season. What do you think?"

"Well, I'll tell you, if I was young I'd do it. You're way ahead of the game — you have a good wagon worth about $1,200 here in Benton, and a team. Wouldn't head out until it gets colder; when you put your bait out you don't want it to spoil. It's going to be a big adventure; you'll freeze your asses off, along with other parts."

"We know. And we figure we might get a couple more freight runs before we head out on our hunt. This would give us time to make plans and get our supplies together."

"One thing, you boys need to be real careful when you go after wolves — don't get near any Indian camps. You kill their dogs and they'll kill you, you'll learn about that."

Jim and John enjoyed their breakfast that morning. Jim told Perkins how they had seen their first buffalo.

"Sure are big. Got all that hair around their head and front shoulder and not much on their butts. Everyone said the best part to eat was the tongue and hump. Been drying and salting tongues and shipping them back east. You ever serve buffalo here at your place? Or does the white man like his beef?"

"Well Jim, we do serve buffalo when we can't get beef, but the trouble is getting someone to go out and shoot them for the meat. Faster to walk a steer up to the back door and put it on your plate. Do you want to bring a buffalo to my place? Not me. Those buffalo can get mean."

Jim and John were able to speak to a freighting clerk that afternoon and learned they could get on the trail the next day going to the mines at Last Chance. It would take about eleven to twelve days to get there, a couple of days to unload, then back. "You might be able to pick up freight there to bring back," the clerk told them. "Then eleven to twelve days back; gotta figure twenty-six to twenty-eight days for the total trip. Same pay: one dollar a day for each of you, plus money for your wagon and team. We'll fix you up with food and grain for the team. You want the trip? We'll get your wagon loaded so you can pull our early tomorrow."

"We sure do want the trip," Jim said, smiling. "Didn't think to get a trip this quick, but that's great, and we know the trail to Last Chance."

"Can we do anything to load, or should I say unload, first?"

"No, boys, we got a good crew here, but we gotta get this freight out of here before the rains start. Freight trails turn to gumbo and you can't move those wagons, but be ready with your team to leave early."

"Thanks," said Jim, shaking the hand of the clerk. "Let's go, John, and get some supplies and get ready for tomorrow. Sure is great heading right out again — or do you want to stick around here a couple of days?"

"Hell no," said John. "You know me, always ready to move on, one day at a time. Enough of Benton, but I'll miss the food at

Perkins'. Let's make sure we eat there tonight, 'cause it's gonna be your and my cooking over buffalo chips the next month."

Jim insisted they feed their team some good grain that afternoon, because he appreciated them more than ever. "After seeing all the teams on the Milk River run, kicking and biting, you see what good, gentle and hard workers we have. Maybe California teams are better."

"You getting lonesome for California, Jim?"

"No, but ask me after one of the winters they keep talking about. Neither of us been here when you talk and your words freeze and fall to the ground."

"That'd be great. Wouldn't hear you all winter! But think of the mess in the spring, cleaning up all them words of yours."

Fort Benton was like a hub on a wagon wheel. Whoop-Up Trail going north, Fish Wagon Road going east, Judith Basin Road and Barker Stage Road going south, and the Mullan Road going west. And all the boats coming up the Missouri; lots of money in freighting.

The trip to Last Chance was slow going because of the big load. One thing was clear to both Jim and John: after seeing the gold mining in California and now in Montana, it was something they wanted to stay away from. Some got rich, but most found no gold or only enough to survive, if that. Now with winter coming on, all digging would have to stop. It made for a wild area around a gold find. Saloons, women and gambling would keep the miners busy, and the prices of food and merchandise were inflated. A man spent months out digging a little gold and could spend it all in one night, then go back out for months just for that one night again in the camp.

On the trip back to Fort Benton the rains started. It was a relief that the wagon was empty, because the more it rained, the deeper the gumbo got. The rims grew twice their size, then three times bigger. The gumbo got so thick on the rims that it started rubbing on the side of the wagon. They got off the wagon to knock the mud off the rims and with every step the gumbo on their boots got bigger. One trip around the wagon and they could hardly lift their boots. With the rain and mud, Jim and John had to sleep in the wagon with those half-rotten hides that they were taking back to Fort Benton. It was also hard to cook. They tried cooking under the wagon but couldn't get anything going. They ate a lot of dried meat and almost no hot food on the trip back.

When they arrived in Fort Benton the rain was starting to change to snow and the ground was freezing at night. They found a room at the hotel, took a hot bath, put on clean clothes, and decided to head for Perkins' for a hot meal.

Jim said, "John, on the way to Perkins' make sure we drop our clothes off at the laundry. Can't take much more of that rotten smell. I don't even want to touch them. How 'bout using the pillow cover, then ask the clerk for a new cover. Tell him you'll return it tomorrow."

"Stick the stuff in the cover and let's get that hot meal."

At the restaurant, Perkins greeted them eagerly, and served them coffee without even asking.

"Damn that tastes good." Jim sat back in his chair with his coffee. "Had one hell of a time trying to cook on this trip. All that rain and mud, feel like you pick up half the earth each time you pick up your foot."

"Well boys, that will stop once the ground starts to freeze. Then your feet feel like they're going to fall off from the cold," said Perkins. "If you're wolfing this winter, you'd better start getting ready with proper clothes and gear."

"We had to sleep with them half-rotten hides on the way back. Boy did we stink. Didn't think I'd ever get that smell off my skin."

"You boys think you smelled when you got back from this trip," said Perkins. "You wait 'till you been wolfing for four or five months with the same clothes and no bath. Remember, no way to wash out there. You come back and we'll be able to smell you clean down the trail like the rest of the trappers. But they say after a month you don't smell yourself anymore."

"Thanks, Perkins. Make sure we come in here first thing we get back before we get a bath. Hate to have you miss out on it," laughed John.

"One thing, you'll be able to clear the place out. Probably close me down."

"Guess we should start getting our supplies together and get out as soon as possible. Sure going to be a new adventure. And if we don't come back in the spring, you can have a service for us," said John.

"We can watch as the Sioux come in to trade and see if your hair is hanging from their scalp rack."

"Nice talk, Perkins. At least we got some hair to give. Looks like you'd be safe out there."

They all laughed.

The meal was delicious and it felt good to get into a real bed that night, though it still seemed to both of them that they were traveling forward in a wagon.

In the morning, Jim and John went over to the Northwest Fur Company. There they could purchase supplies and also get a buyer for their furs. The clerk greeted them.

"We plan to go wolfing this winter," Jim said. "We need clothes and supplies. You have any suggestions for us?"

"Sure do, boys. We'll fix you up with everything you need and we'll buy your pelts for top dollar in the spring. We'll get you started for one hundred dollars per man. Pants over there, boots on the wall. Start trying them on; make sure the buffalo coats are plenty big so you can put many layers under. I'll get you strychnine and ammo for your rifle and side arms. A couple of men with a gun and a little strychnine make themselves 'bout three thousand dollars or more in a season. We pay a dollar and a half to three dollars for wolves, red fox two dollars, gray fox or coyote about a dollar each. We also buy muskrat, otter, bear, elk and antelope.

"Take a look at them wolf pelts. You get more if you slit the wolf hides down the belly from the chin to the root of the tail and inside of each leg to intersect with the belly cut. If you do this, the tail slips off the bone and you get a complete pelt. Remember, good pelt, more money.

"Since the weather's starting to change, you should get out and locate some buffalo.

"Take lots of salt for the hides; beans, flour, coffee for you. You'll get all the fresh meat you need out there."

Jim said, "Looks like we got all we need. Here's the money. We'll bring the wagon around to pick it up."

"Good luck, boys. It's going to be a long winter for you," the clerk said.

That night Perkins told them how to cook buffalo hump and tongue.

"You boil the buffalo tongue for a long time. Then you can eat it sliced or slice it and fry it. The hump you cook like a roast in a Dutch oven or you can slice it and fry it like a steak. It's also good roasted over a fire. You boys getting ready to leave soon?"

"Tomorrow," explained John.

"All I can say is make sure you have plenty of ammunition, coffee and salt. You'll be sleeping on the prairie like the rest of the animals. Ain't much shelter from the storm. Find a wash-out on a river bank. It's going to be a big adventure for you boys, sure wish I was younger and could go with you," Perkins said with a big smile.

"That was the best meal we've had here. You really come through. How much do we owe you?"

"Nothing, Jim — this one's on me. Just want you to remember how good my food is so you want to come back. And one last word of advice for you boys. Don't get none of those Indians mad at you. I'd hate to send half a man back to Indiana to be buried. Good luck — see you in the spring."

"Thanks again, Perkins. As they say, you'll probably smell us before you see us," said Jim.

CHAPTER THREE

The Wolf Hunt

NEVER HAD JIM SEEN so much vast, treeless country; just miles of that Montana buffalo grass. And that crazy wind. Warm for awhile, then a couple of days later it changed direction and blew cold.

"I'm ready to set up camp and get some fresh meat," John said to his brother.

"They say antelope's the easiest game to kill; they're curious. All you have to do is sit down and they approach, moving closer and closer. You pick the one you want as they come around," Jim said.

"I've heard that story," laughed John. "If that doesn't work, fall on your back and kick your feet. But just make sure you go for a small one. Also remember they start bunching into a large band. This is when we go after their hides."

As they moved farther out onto the plain, the abundance of game amazed them. A day didn't go by when they weren't able to spot elk, antelope, mountain sheep, deer, wolf or bear. And they were never out of sight of the huge herds of buffalo. The slow, even-paced wagon never seemed to disturb the buffalo; where they grazed Jim also saw great numbers of wolves waiting for a calf or old buffalo to become separated from the herd. Then the wolves circled, biting at the legs and throat of the animal, slowly making it weaker and weaker.

At last Jim and John made their camp at the Missouri River, halfway between the Judith River and the Milk River. It was well sheltered from cold winds and had a good water supply. They cut wood and stored their provisions. The weather was turning very cold, only a little warmth emanating now from the mid-day sun. It was only the middle of November and already they had seen some light snows.

Once the camp was in place it was time to head out and kill some buffalo for bait. They had passed encampments of Gros Ventres along the Judith and remembered the advice they had been given: "Keep the poisoned buffalo away from Indian camps." They planned to make a large circle in the other direction that they could cover in four or five days, then head back to the base camp. This was different from the way most trappers and hunters did it; most just kept on the move and had no base. Jim had to hope no Indians or other trappers found their camp and stole or destroyed their hides.

The boys killed twenty buffalo in their first circle and were back in camp in six days. They spent a day in camp and then started on their trip to retrieve the wolves. At the first baited buffalo, they had twelve wolves and it took three hours to prepare the hides. By the time they had made the circle they had 200 wolf pelts; it took ten days.

As the weather grew colder and the snowstorms stronger, it took longer to make the circle. New bait had to be prepared and they found that the circle had to be drawn in. But by the end of December they had 1800 wolf pelts, and also many pelts from bear, deer and elk.

Then, as the weather worsened, more time had to be spent in camp just trying to keep from freezing.

"John, we got a wagon full of pelts. I'm not feeling so good. Must be mid-January. I think we ought to start back for Benton."

"You getting a cold or what?" said John. "We could load the wagon and be out of here in a couple of days."

As they started breaking camp, Jim felt weak. He started to run a fever. Later in the morning he was delirious. John had a hard time getting him into the wagon.

The snowdrifts were high but the ground was frozen and the wagon was able to move. John looked at his brother and thought: in fourteen or fifteen days, by the time we get back to Benton, Jim will be dead. He had gone from a little chill, to a fever, to delirious in just a day. John continued to wrap his brother in blankets but Jim threw them off and tried to climb out of the wagon. John couldn't make more than fifteen miles his first day. The team was running out of feed and John gave them a few oats. He hoped they could dig in the snow and find some grass. He saw that the team would weaken if he kept pushing them.

Jim screamed and talked that first long night. John forced him to drink some melted snow. He felt lonely and afraid.

Next morning he thought: we'll get the team hooked up and get started on this second day of hell. It's starting to snow again. At least when it snows it isn't so cold.

Then he thought: maybe if I push it I can make it to that Indian camp near the Judith. At least I could get Jim inside if they don't kill me for the furs. I have to take a chance. I know he will never make it all the way to Benton. I'll stop in this little draw for the night, see if I can make that Indian camp tomorrow. I gotta get some food into Jim. Can break some of these dead bushes along this wash, use a little coal oil, get a little fire going. I'll boil some dried meat and give Jim the juice.

Please Jim, just drink a little. I don't want you to die on me out here. Jim, I'll get you to that Indian camp tomorrow if I gotta kill that team.

Third day out. I ought to be able to find that camp, John thought; should see smoke. Damn this day's almost gone and still no camp. Wait, I think I see something. Just hope it's the Gros Ventres and someone will be able to understand me. Starting to get dark. Only a little bit more.

John approached the camp with his wagon and team. Not much activity. Everyone was inside the tipis.

"Hello?" he called. "Someone's gotta be willing to come out and talk to me."

Just then a tipi flap went back and a Gros Ventre walked out. He looked ten feet tall and huge with his buffalo robe.

John knew this man was the chief. "My brother is very sick. I need help." John started to worry that the man wouldn't understand him. "My brother very sick!"

"I heard you the first time," the Gros Ventre said. "You tell me why I should give you help. You are out killing all our game so that we will starve."

"Please," John pleaded. "Just look at him. He's my brother and I don't know what to do and I will pay."

The Indian looked at Jim. He said, "I know this man. He gave me some blankets and ammunition for my rifle." He turned back to John. "I am called Horse Capture, the leader of this band."

"I'm John Wells and this is my brother Jim. I'm worried that he's gone loco in the head. I don't think he's going to make it."

"Bring him into my tipi," Horse Capture said. "Don't take

his buffalo robe off too fast; you must warm him slowly. And you, go to my brother's lodge and sleep." He pointed to a tipi about three away. "I will take care of your team."

John had a quick thought that this was the end for himself and his team.

"I will get Bull Lodge, our medicine man, to look at your brother. Now go."

John was so tired he walked over to the tipi and pulled the flap back. Inside was a buck, his squaw and two children, a boy about ten and a girl maybe eight. He didn't know how but it seemed they were waiting for him. It was impossible since the big Indian hadn't talked to anyone.

The buck pointed to where John was to sit and handed him a bowl of something like a thick soup. He didn't care what it was — it was hot, it tasted good and it was filling. He tried to talk but no one seemed to understand him. He was starting to get warm and sleepy so he took off his buffalo coat. The Indian woman pointed to a pile of robes, put her hands to her head and closed her eyes as if to say, "You sleep there."

The tipi was warm and sleep came fast. John felt himself trying to wake a couple of times during the night, but it was the first time he had been warm in months and the weight of sleep took over.

In the morning, the tipi was empty but the fire still burned. John stuck his head through the flap and looked outside. It was mid-morning; the snow had stopped falling and the day felt warm. He pulled himself back in and was putting on his buffalo robe and boots when the Indian woman returned with a friendly smile. She sat down by the fire, took some stuff out of a big pot and placed it in a small pan. She put it over the fire and motioned to John to sit down. It wasn't long before the stuff was boiling. She poured it into a bowl and gave it to him. Again, it was hot, tasted good and was filling. She also handed John a piece of what looked like bread, but it was heavy and hard. It tasted like stale bread in which the flour hadn't been ground, but by dipping it in his bowl it became soft and gained a little taste. She also gave him a cup of hot liquid that tasted the way the sagebrush smelled.

John was anxious to see how his brother was fairing. He had some supplies he would share with this woman when he could make it out to his wagon, but first he wanted to see Jim. At last, when he finished his food, he smiled and thanked her and walked out to the tipi that Jim had been taken into the night before. On his way over he could see the wagon and team. The horses had been hobbled.

John opened the flap and was greeted by the Chief. But Jim wasn't there. His heart sank.

Horse Capture saw the look on John's face and said, "Don't worry; he is with our medicine man at the sweat lodge."

"Can I go and see him?" John asked.

"Yes, I will take you."

They walked a short distance to a low lodge. It looked like a hole covered by a half-round roof laid with many buffalo robes. A fire crackled in the rocks near the lodge.

"We must wait until the medicine man opens the lodge. We must not disrupt the sweat," said Horse Capture.

John could hear chanting from inside. For nearly ten minutes he stood outside and listened. Then a very old man came out, heavy with sweat. He walked over to the cold stream and sat down, covering himself with the icy cold water. John's mouth must have dropped because Capture said, "It is good for you to sweat and then cool in the stream. Come, let's see your brother. The medicine man is trying to break his fever."

When John bent over to enter the dark, hot sweat lodge, he could see Jim lying naked on a buffalo robe. He looked weak and sick. And he was still delirious, moving in crazy ways.

"John, your brother is very sick," explained Capture. Putting a hand on John's shoulder, he said, "The medicine man will do one more sweat, then I will move him back to my lodge. My daughter will feed him and hope the fever will leave and not make him weak for life. Do you want to sweat with him? If you do, take off all your clothes and put them just outside the lodge. Sit by your brother and the medicine man will be back."

"I want to stay with him," said John.

John took off his clothes and set them in a pile outside. The cold wind caught him and caused him to draw back. He could see the medicine man returning from the river, steam rising from every part of his body. He carried a large container of water in his hands. He entered the lodge, bent over and sat down, not saying a word. Soon some Indians came in with rocks from the fire, held between two wooden poles; they stacked them in a depression in the center of the lodge. When about ten rocks were stacked, the Indians left and closed the flap. John could feel the heat from the rocks and thought how nice and warm it was.

Just then the old medicine man started to chant. He chanted for a couple of minutes, then poured water on the hot rocks. John felt the hot flash of steam hit his face and the temperature in the lodge start to rise. As more water splashed the rocks it became harder to breathe. He thought he would run but held himself. "God," he thought, "it can't get any hotter." When he thought he would scream, the flap of the lodge opened and cold air relieved him. The old medicine man stood and walked out, heading again for the stream. John followed him.

The ice had been cut back so they could walk out to their waists and sit. The water didn't sting; it was refreshing. Not only did John realize then that he and his brother were not in danger, but that he had no choice but to leave him there to get well. The trip to Fort Benton would kill him. The hardest part was deciding whether to stay there himself.

In less than a minute John followed the medicine man out of the stream, back to the pile of clothing outside the sweat lodge. John put on his clothes and buffalo coat, and the old medicine man put on his robes.

John looked in. They had already taken Jim back to the tipi, so he headed over that way. He had never felt so refreshed and clean in his life. As he walked over he thought, "I've had my first sweat, but not my last."

Inside the tipi Capture told him, "John, your brother is sleeping and now we leave the medicine to the women. Come sit down and have something to drink. You must drink a lot after a sweat."

"You do that a lot?" asked John.

"It is the way we clear our mind and body. I like it once a day but sometimes it is not possible. The best is to sweat in the evening before I sleep. It makes sleep much better."

"How long does the medicine man believe my brother will take to become well?" John asked.

Horse Capture said, "He does not know. It may take the winter before he can travel again safely."

"Tomorrow, then, I will leave," said John. "You don't need another one of us around all winter to take care of. I will pay you for my brother's care and supply you with all the food I won't need. In fact, I will give you Jim's horse as part payment."

"I trust you, John. If he should die I want you to know we did try to heal him."

"I know that, Capture, and I will try to get back with some help."

"You do have something we would like — the deer and antelope hides. We can cure them during the winter and I'm willing to trade other hides for them."

"I have about fifty and you can have them. They look much better when you tan them than when the whites do. Yours are so soft and brown; ours are white and stiff. I'll sell the rest of what I have in Fort Benton when I try to bring back help for Jim. It shouldn't take me more than fourteen days to get back."

"It will depend on the weather. The weather can be good like now but in a short time grows very cold and the snows come," explained Capture.

"I still think I should leave tomorrow and try to get through. I feel good that Jim is with you and I know you will do all you can for him. But I also know that he would never make it to Fort Benton. I want to check on him."

John saw that Jim was sleeping quietly. As he sat by him he was able to get a good look at the lodge. This lodge was a little larger than most; it was made of buffalo hides and was sewn together with sinew. The lodge equipment was nicely laid out on a buffalo robe. He could see knives, both of bone and of metal, kettles, horn spoons, fleshing tools and food containers of all sorts. He could see bladders hung full of water and large containers full of dried buffalo meat and other foods. The lodge was clean and neat. He felt he had made the right choice in leading Jim here, and that they had been lucky in meeting this band before. He would go out to the wagon and give them what they wanted. Thank God that Capture spoke English and there seemed to have been some contact with the missionaries.

John walked over to his wagon and started taking down the things he wanted to leave. He unloaded the deer and antelope hides, two heavy blankets, fifty pounds of flour, two sacks of sugar, one saddle horse and a whole frozen antelope. He called Capture over and showed him the pile of goods. Capture said he would take care of the distribution of the supplies.

A feast was arranged for John that night and he ate well, not asking what. He woke early the next morning to check on Jim. It would be hard to leave him like this, but he felt he was doing the right thing.

John felt very lonesome when he left the camp. It was the first time in a long while the two brothers had been separated, and it was big brother Jim who was supposed to be taking care of John, not the other way around. Damn! He hated to make this trip by himself.

CHAPTER FOUR

With the Gros Ventres

CAPTURE'S DAUGHTER, MORNING STAR, was sixteen years old. She should have been married but she had stayed with a family near Fort Benton to be educated. A girl could not menstruate until after she had experienced sexual intercourse — if she started before then, her family would be disgraced. Morning Star had been an exception. She liked helping with this white man. Her father had told the medicine man: "I do not want this white man to die."

Bull Lodge instructed Morning Star: "I have stripped the bark of the willow and boiled it. I want you to give him a half-cup every time you can. The willow should break the fever. I also want you to put grease of the buffalo on his chest — keep him wrapped in buffalo robes. Do not let him uncover himself. You must also boil meat and feed him the juice, and break bones and put the juice of the bones in. Someone must be with him at all times." Bull Lodge spoke with much authority. "You can also put cool water on his head."

The white man was handsome but very sick. He continually threw off his robe. Sometimes she let it slip away for a moment before she pulled it back over him. He had a battle scar on his left shoulder — she wondered how it happened.

All the girls she had been raised with were now married, many with children. Some had even been married twice. When they married older men the husbands would die; then when they were widowed early in their lives, remarriage was quickly arranged. Their husband's brother had first claim. Maggie felt she was lucky; she had only known one family, but many older women were widowed three or four times, giving them three or four different families.

She wondered, looking at Jim, why she imagined that he was a good and kind man. Many of the Indian women who married whites were not treated well, and the men who had Indian wives were ridiculed in Fort Benton.

For four years she took care of the Walsh children. Mr. Walsh was in the Army and seemed to be a leader. She was able to go to school and was treated like part of the family. She went to church with the family and was baptized a Catholic and given a Christian name: "Margaret," or "Maggie" for short. She was registered with the last name "Walsh." Maggie Walsh — her white name. When she went places with the Walsh family she was treated well, although more than once she had heard Mr. Walsh explaining to somebody in town that she wasn't a "typical" Indian. But Morning Star had become Maggie Walsh without difficulty, as she was intelligent and eager to try new things. By the time she returned to her tribe, she knew she wanted to choose the man she married like the white girls did.

Jim was moaning. He was swinging his arms and rolling around. Morning Star was frightened and called to her mother for help. The two of them held him down and kept him wrapped. After a few minutes, he went back to sleep. So Morning Star just sat back and continued to watch him. The battle between life and death went on for many days.

Morning Star, like all Gros Ventres, valued life very highly and prayed for a long one. She prayed for Jim, both as a Christian and as a Gros Ventre. He should not die alone. If he were to die, he must be surrounded by family and friends. She felt he had only one friend, and she was it.

The medicine man had not given up hope. If he had, he would have dressed Jim in the best clothes they had available, combing his hair, painting his face.

If he died they would wash his corpse and it would be the last time she would see that snow-white body.

She kept thinking: what would they do with his body? Would he be treated like a Gros Ventre? Would he be placed, dressed, on a blanket, in a place of honor in the back of his father's lodge, then wrapped in a robe, put on two carrying poles and put in the fork of a tree with his head toward the setting sun?

The Gros Ventres never put the body in the ground like the whites. If you were not put in a tree, you could be placed on a knoll and a structure like a sweat lodge built over you to protect you from wild animals. Or you could be set in the cleft of a cliff and covered with rocks. But if you were a leader like her father, your own lodge would be your resting place. If this was done, holes would be dug in which the lodge poles were placed. This made the structure more permanent. Your body would be placed in the lodge along with your best furnishings. The door of the lodge would be closed, the cover pegged down, and everything secured as well as it could be.

Morning Star started to cry. These were not happy thoughts. Jim would live and her father too would have a long life.

-□-

John travelled about three days out from the Indian camp and was hit with one of the worst storms he had ever been in. The temperature dropped so low he found a draw, put the wagon on top, and crawled in the draw with the horses. He was able to find some dry deadwood and get a fire going. He fed the horses some oats, hobbled them, and settled himself the best he could for a long storm. At least he could melt snow and make hot coffee. He was lonesome, cold, tired and dirty. If he froze, he would at least keep until spring.

"How in the hell them horses can stick their noses down in the snow and find grass is amazing," he thought. "But these animals really do survive out here. If I make it," he thought, "I'm never going to spend another winter out in the open. Jim and I have done some crazy things, but this was the worst."

Jim seemed to be improving. He had spells when he was awake but was still very weak. He had been in the lodge for almost seven days. A big storm had been raging for four days and had kept everyone in, so Morning Star had not been alone with Jim. But this storm would be over in a couple more days, and at least Jim was going to live. As he got better she would be with him more as the other women went back to their tasks.

They were still feeding him the broth with carrots. All had to be mashed so he wouldn't choke. Morning Star was given the task of feeding him. She would put his head on her lap and slowly tip the cup. The broth wasn't enough — he had lost weight. When he was strong enough to know where he was, she would cook him lots of Indian bread to put the fat back on him.

On the ninth day, Jim opened his eyes and tried to talk. He sat up against her father's back rest for a short time. But he had no strength and had to lie down after a very short time.

She was feeding him when he spoke his first words: "You are very beautiful." She almost dropped the broth, but pretended not to understand and continued to feed him. But a strange feeling came across her. It was good to see some life in his eyes. He looked at her again and tried to speak, but no words came out. She laid him down and he went right back to sleep.

The next morning Jim seemed stronger but he had developed a heavy cough. Her mother took some clay, made it damp with warm water, wrapped it in a cloth with some herbs, and put it on his chest. She kept hot packs on his chest at all times.

When Morning Star was feeding Jim again that day, he spoke: "I know you don't understand me, but you are very beautiful. I feel I have died and entered a new world, a world with such beauty." He closed his eyes. "I must learn the language so I can communicate," he thought.

Horse Capture came in to speak with Jim. "I'm pleased you are still with us, Jim. You have been a very sick man. Your brother brought you to us almost ten days ago. He has gone to Fort Benton and will return for you. You are our guest and we will take care of you."

Jim opened his eyes and said, "Thank you," then dozed off again.

The next day he showed more strength and was given more food. Not too much, as it would make him sick. A new soup was prepared for him. It was a soup that made children healthy. It was made with marrow, guts and rose berries. The skin had peeled off his chest and it was very sore where the hot clay had been rubbed. One of the Indian women put a mixture of herbs and tallow on the burns.

That afternoon he was given his first bath. He was rubbed with snow. They powdered him like a baby with powder made from buffalo chips that were pounded on rawhide and sterilized with hot stones. This powder was put on all parts of his body. It felt good, and not knowing what the powder was, he didn't care.

Capture came back in the afternoon, and Jim was able to talk to him without tiring.

Capture told Jim he was at the Judith River in the Indians' winter camp. He said a big storm had been raging for days and everyone was waiting for a break to get out for a few hours.

Jim napped again that afternoon, and when he awoke the beautiful Indian girl was sitting at his side, ready to help him eat. Jim looked at her and said, "It is such a great thing to open my eyes and see a person as lovely as you. I only wish I could talk to you. I can't get over how kind you are."

Morning Star could feel the blood fill her face, but she kept a straight face and put the bowl of soup in front of him. She held a spoonful out and put it to his lips, and watched as he accepted each bite. She noticed that her hand was shaking. She dipped a piece of bread in the soup and gave it to Jim. As she looked at him, she thought how nice his beard was. She wanted to touch it as she had when he was ill, but now she dared not reach out and touch him, no matter how much she wanted to.

That evening Jim was able to sit up for a while. Morning Star watched the fire casting shadows on Jim's face while her father talked with him; she still wanted to go over and touch him.

The next morning she started to menstruate and was so embarrassed she left her lodge and went to the lodge of her uncle, where she would stay for the next five days. It would be almost impossible to stay away from Jim that long, but she must.

Jim spent the whole next day waiting for the beautiful girl

to appear, and finally that evening he asked Horse Capture what had happened to her. "Oh," Capture said, "you mean my daughter. She is sick and at the lodge of my brother."

"What's her name?" asked Jim.

"Morning Star. She is my first child, a very strong girl who should be married by now. She is sixteen and says she will make her own choice. That is not our way. The choice should be made for her and should have been made four or five years ago. Now she is getting old. I love her very much," he shook his head, "but as I said, she is the first woman I have no control over. It is very bad if she does not get a husband."

"You know," said Jim, "our women very seldom marry before they are sixteen, and some turn twenty-one, or even more, so you shouldn't worry."

Jim was gaining his strength each day. He was able to put on his clothes, which the Indian women had washed. He even put his head out of the tipi. Still snowing hard. It had been four days since he had seen Morning Star, and he hoped she wasn't too sick and that he would see her soon.

The next day the storm ended and at last the sun was out. Jim left the tipi for the first time. He was weak in the knees and tired fast. He still had the bad cough and was spitting up some blood. That evening, when they all sat to eat, he looked up and Morning Star was there across from him. He broke into a big smile and said out loud, "I missed you and hope you're feeling much better." Then he felt silly, knowing she didn't understand him.

She said simply, "Thank you, and I hope you are feeling much better too."

Jim nearly fell over. "You speak — ? Why didn't you say something?"

Morning Star smiled and said, "I wanted you to speak more."

"Where did you learn?" Jim asked.

"With a family at Fort Benton. I took care of the children and attended school. The family's name was Walsh. I was baptized and given a Christian name, Margaret Walsh. All the children call me 'Maggie,' so if you want you can also call me Maggie."

"Damn," said Jim again. "Here I thought your father was the only one who spoke English. I want to learn to speak your language. Will you teach me?"

"Our language is very hard. You should learn the language of the Blackfeet, and I can teach you their tongue. It is much easier, and spoken by many."

"I sure look forward to you being my teacher. Can we start early tomorrow?"

"Yes, we can," smiled Maggie.

It took John until the second week in February to finally reach Fort Benton. He and his team were half-starved, but he did make it. The first thing he did was take the wagon to I.G. Baker's and tell the clerk to unload it and count the furs. Then he took his team over to the stable and told the stable boy to treat them with care.

He staggered over to the hotel and ordered a room with a bath. He peeled off his stinking clothes and climbed into the tub. It was the first time he had been warm since the sweat. "This is the life," John thought. "No more of that open country." All he had hoped was to survive.

After the water cooled he pulled himself out and put on some fresh clothes. He wanted to go to Perkins' and eat everything in the place. Stepping out of the hotel, he again realized how cold it was. Mr. Perkins looked up with a big smile when John walked in; a worried look played across his face when he didn't see Jim.

"Where's your brother?" Perkins said, as he shook John's hand.

"Get me a big cup of coffee and I'll tell you the story," John said as he sat down. "And please cook me up a big meal."

Perkins brought over the coffee and sat down with John.

"Well," John started, "we got some good hunting in from the end of October into December. But Jim took sick. He got a fever and went out of his head. I was sure he was going to die. I put him in a wagon and started back for Benton. But I knew we couldn't make it. I ran into a band of Gros Ventre Indians near the Judith River. Damn this is good coffee! — I've been drinking ground buffalo chips when I could find them. I asked if I could leave Jim with them. I gave them supplies and some hides. I know Jim can make it. I been trying to get back here for weeks, damn near killed my team and froze my ass. Left the hides at Baker's. Got to the hotel, took a bath. Now I'm here, and that's 'bout my story."

"Good to see you alive, John. Think you did the right thing for your brother. The Gros Ventres can be good friends," Perkins said. "In fact, a girl stayed with an officer's family over at the Fort on and off last three or four years. He left this fall and she's back with her tribe. Smart girl. Traders like to work with them because they tan their hides the best."

"I gotta get back, I promised Jim," John said, thinking about what he had just been through.

"Jim should be in good hands," Perkins said. "Their doctoring is better than some of ours. You're not going to be able to get back before spring."

"But I promised."

"Don't even think about it. He'd rather see you alive in the spring."

The first thing John did in the morning was head for Baker's to see what he would get for the hides.

"Morning, Mr. Wells. Hope you had a good rest. Got your hides all counted and separated. 'Course you want to know what they're worth. Good hides, first of the year. Boss says sixty-eight hundred, that's a fair price. If you want you can try the other traders, but that's fair price."

"I heard you the first time. I ain't deaf," John said. "Sounds good. Happy to get rid of them. But I got one favor to ask. I'd like to leave my wagon out back of your store. I won't need it for a while."

"I'm sure it'll be fine. I'll have the boys push it out back," the clerk responded.

"I'll collect the money from you later," John said as he walked out the door.

It's going to be a long winter for me here in Fort Benton.

Jim couldn't wait for the next day to be with Maggie and start his lessons. He wanted to know all he could about these people. But for now he was feeling tired and just wanted to sleep.

He woke to the sound of the preparation of the morning meal. Today he wanted to know what he was eating; or maybe, he thought, he shouldn't know.

He watched Maggie helping the other women.

Horse Capture came in with another Indian who was dressed differently and seemed also to have the power of a leader. He was introduced to Jim as Bull Lodge, the medicine man who had doctored him. Jim thanked him for all his help and consideration — Capture translating. The two men had a long conversation; Capture put his hand on Jim's shoulder and said, "The medicine man is very happy with his healing powers on you. He feels that the Great Spirit wanted you to live so you will be able to help us someday, but you must be careful and get your strength back."

They both smiled and knew that a lasting friendship was developing.

That afternoon was Jim's first lesson about the Gros Ventres. Maggie sat across from him and said, "Where do you want to start?"

Jim said, "I want a little history and to learn a few words."

She started with a story. "My people tell a story of finding a sacred waterfall that had healing powers. The water came out of the mountain and would flow in great amounts, then stop for a period of time, then flow again. If you bathed in this water you could cure many of the health problems my people had. The whites called the mountain the Salt River Range. It was far below the area where the mud boiled and hot water came from the ground. I would like to see this place sometime. Our tribe liked the Blackfeet but did not like the traders and fur hunters. But we soon realized that the traders were here to stay. The American Fur Company wanted to trade with us because we were known by all as better dressers of buffalo robes than any other tribe. As you know, the value of fur changes. When we first started to trade with the fort they wanted beaver skins, and one beaver skin was worth two buffalo robes. But our tribe didn't kill beaver. Beaver lessened in value and finally three or four beaver skins became equal to one buffalo robe. So as the buffalo robes went up in value, the more the traders wanted to trade with us."

"How about a few words," Jim said.

"Jim Wells, batz-zatz," Maggie said.

"What does that mean?"

"It means you are good and strong," she laughed.

As the days went on, Jim grew stronger and was able to speak a little of the Blackfoot language. But it was hard since everyone around him spoke Gros Ventre, so he still couldn't understand the common conversation.

He looked forward to the time with Maggie and wanted to get outside so he could be alone with her. He felt himself falling in love with her, but he kept remembering that he was eleven years older than she was. Then again, Gros Ventre women married older men — married! What was he thinking? Marry an Indian whom he barely knew, whose life was completely different? Or was it so different? It was the first time in his life he could say that he had felt love for a woman — no, girl — no, woman. She was a woman.

Jim wanted to write down his experiences but didn't have paper or pen. How would he remember it all? Being part of a tribe, seeing how a family was a family and how these people ate and slept. They were no longer savages to him, but people of flesh and blood. And he was falling in love with one. He could feel deep down that he wanted to spend the rest of his life with Maggie. He kept fighting this thought. Wasn't it just because he was here? It would change once he left, wouldn't it? No, he was in love.

As the days went on it became harder for him not to reach over and take her hand, but he was going to do everything possible to be proper, and not let them lose respect for him. He was their guest, and a long-staying guest at that.

Jim wanted to ask Maggie about the custom of eating dog, and one day he finally did.

She laughed. "You've already eaten dog, when I bring those fresh pinkish chunks of meat into the tipi. Buffalo meat is first but dog meat is second. The flesh of grown dogs is eaten only in times of famine. The nursing pups are a delicacy. The pups are to us like chicken is to you whites, and this is why you see so many female dogs in our camp."

Jim said, "So that pork-like odor that's cooking over the fire, making that delicious stew, tasting like young pig, is really young dog, and a treat for honored guests?"

"Yes," she said simply.

"I'm glad that I fully enjoyed that delicious stew of pups before I knew what I was eating."

"Buffalo is our main source of food, dog our treat, then additional meat comes from elk, deer and antelope. We eat beaver, prairie dogs, gophers and all kinds of rabbit; all of these are hunted and trapped by children, not adults. We eat some birds and their eggs, such as duck, goose, grouse, and prairie chicken, and we will eat badger and porcupine, young wolves and coyote. We never eat full-grown wolf, coyote, fox, mountain lion, lynx, bobcat or otter. Bear is only killed if a hunter comes across one; the flesh is eaten and the grease is good. We are not that much different from you. The only thing you would not eat is dog, wolf, coyote and fox. But you do eat the rest and would eat these if hungry."

"You're right," Jim said. "I could eat dog now and it wouldn't bother me."

It was hard for Jim not to wonder what he was eating at each meal. But he could feel his health coming back a little more every day.

One day Maggie brought Jim a new set of clothes made from deerskin. The shirt was hand-beaded with some embroidery. This would be the buckskin he would wear as long as he lived in the territory. The pants were beautifully made, and as he put them on, he couldn't believe how well they fit.

"Who made these?" Jim asked.

"I did," said Maggie, with her eyes cast down, an embarrassed red in her cheeks.

"These are the most wonderful clothes and gifts I have ever had. How did you do all this?"

"The clothes are made from the skins you gave my people, and I worked on them when you were so sick," Maggie smiled. "I have also made you a cap and mittens of beaver skin for the winter."

"I have nothing as a gift to you, and you have done so much for me, Maggie, not only you but your family. You have become like my family." Tears came to Jim's eyes. "I will never be able to repay you for saving my life."

Maggie felt so close to Jim she had to leave the lodge.

Jim didn't want her to leave and felt his hand go out to stop her, but she was gone. He couldn't believe how well the buckskin fit, how good and warm it felt, the smooth golden brown color of it. He didn't see Maggie the rest of that day or at the evening meal.

It always amazed him how the Indians did so much with so little, and how neat the tipis were kept. When he was first able to sit up he used a very fancy back rest, which must have belonged to Capture. Now he had his own back rest and all extra robes were hung in back of the chair to keep the cold out. He wondered if he could work out a life with Maggie. He kept trying to stop these thoughts because of all the obstacles. He was white, she was Indian; he was twenty-seven years old, she was only sixteen. Yet she was so mature and responsible. Also, she was educated in white schools. With all these thoughts he didn't know if she had any feeling for him.

When spring came he would go to Fort Benton and try to get a job with the American Fur Company. After a winter with these Indians he would be able to trade with them. He would like to have his own trading post. If he could establish himself he could think about marrying and settling down, and if he stayed out here he could marry Maggie because it would be acceptable. If she loved him too. He was happy being in the village, living, eating, sleeping there, learning to speak the language. "It's funny," Jim thought, "my brother left me here so sick, he doesn't know if I'm dead or alive. Well, I'm alive and in love. Wait until he sees me. What a surprise all this will be."

There were breaks in the weather and Jim was able to get out and walk some. He was still weak, and his cough came back occasionally to plague him, but most of his strength had returned. Soon he was able to do a little riding and hunting so he could provide some fresh meat for the camp. The funny thing was going to Capture to borrow his own horse, which John had turned over to the Gros Ventres. It had become a joke between Capture and Jim.

The camp was expecting an early spring, which would bring the buffalo back from the south on their way to Canada.

Maggie had told him he would see great things this spring when the buffalo came back across the Missouri River and the ice started to break up on the river.

One morning, Jim woke up to wailing sounds coming from one of the tipis. An old man had died during the night. He had been a leader and was respected and loved. When Jim had been introduced to him, he looked small and fragile. He had told Jim how he valued life and had always prayed to the Great Spirit for a long one, which had been granted to him. But he had been ready and resigned to death. He had given all the instructions to his family and friends on how he wanted to be disposed.

Jim went over to pay his respects to the family, and found the old man on a buffalo robe in his finest clothes, hair combed and face painted. It made Jim feel good to see the respect the man was given, and to know that the Indians had the same feelings as the whites. Chanting and prayers went on all morning. Shortly after noon the body was wrapped and taken out and placed in a tree, with the head toward the setting sun.

Jim was included in the ceremonies and was made to feel comfortable. He attended a sweat at least once a week. The sweat not only promoted health by cleansing the body, but was also very spiritual. All sweat lodges, Jim learned, were constructed the same way, about nine feet in diameter, with a large entrance facing east and another open to the west. On the north and south of the circle, fifteen willows were stuck in the ground. The number thirty was always used. These thirty willows were arched over and woven into a ridge willow that ran east to west.

The ridge pole willow was painted black with charcoal. The thirty side willows were also painted black, but only from where the upright sections began to arch to the top. All the painting was done by rubbing charcoal on the hands and then sliding the pole through the blackened hands. After the framework was up and painted, it was covered with robes so it was airtight.

Inside the sweat lodge, a pit was dug in the center, about two feet square and sixteen inches deep. This pit was filled with heated rocks.

The ground was cleared of grass and smoothed, so that hides could be placed on it.

Sagebrush was sprinkled around the inside of the sweat lodge next to the wall. The sage added a wonderful smell and could be rubbed on the body during the sweat.

The main entrance of the lodge was on a line with the east-west axis of the sweat lodge. About ten feet out was a hearth and fire for heating the rocks. Still farther out, on the same axis, about twenty-five feet from the lodge, was a mound or altar. It was set with different symbols, the skull of a buffalo, the sacred pipe, or the feathers and claws of the eagle. The altar or mound was built from the dirt from the pit in the sweat lodge.

The thing that amazed Jim was the use of pipes in many rituals. The two pipes he was learning the most about were the Flat Pipe and the Feathered Pipe. He was told by Horse Capture, "The Flat Pipe belongs on the ground, or on the surface of the earth. The Flat Pipe is only smoked when it is being transferred to a new keeper, and is never danced with. The Feathered Pipe is smoked a great deal, and dancing with it is common."

Jim watched each ritual. Movement was always clockwise. There was lots of singing, which the Gros Ventres loved to do anytime. Painted buffalo chips were used for the fire. The buffalo chips burned very hot and the ash was clean. Sage, tobacco, and wild parsley were put into the fire to add an aroma.

The keeper of the Pipe was Lame Bull. Jim asked him how he was chosen for this role. Lame Bull told him the story.

When he was a young man, he vowed never to become keeper of either the Flat or the Feathered Pipe, since being a keeper meant having a complicated and difficult life. He concentrated on becoming a warrior, and remained free.

When he was in his mid-twenties and had three wives, he was asleep one night when an old woman came to his tipi and woke him. She was warning him that a crowd was on the way to his lodge to make him keeper of the Pipe.

He quickly mounted his horse and took off for the mountains, but while he was gone all his belongings were taken by the crowd. And then the old keeper of the Pipe started to perform the rite for summoning unwilling people.

Lame Bull was hiding up in the mountains with his horses. He did not want to give his horses away, as he would be required to do as keeper. So while he listened to the singing and rattling of the rite down below, he determined that they could sing forever, but that he would never come down.

The rite went on. At last he looked at his horses again and thought, "I have plenty of horses. Surely they won't make me get rid of all of them. I think I'll go down and become keeper. Probably they have my wives by now anyway, and my children will need me."

So he came down off the mountain and galloped all the way back to camp. The old keeper still had the Flat Pipe in his hands. Lame Bull took the Pipe, and went through the whole rite and became keeper. The rite cost him, among other things, a total of thirty horses. All through his life, Lame Bull thought that being summoned by the Flat Pipe from a distance of a couple of miles was one of his greatest experiences.

It was Jim's intent to learn all he could about the beliefs of the Gros Ventres.

The Gros Ventres believed in a "Supreme Being" or "The One Above." He was prayed to in the sweat lodge through the grandfathers, or the tribe members who had died. He had no wife or children; in fact he had no body, and never took on a material form. He never appeared to a person in a dream or vision either.

Jim thought that their God sounded a lot like his.

Maggie told Jim a story about when the first priest came to the Gros Ventres. They thought he was the Supreme Being who had descended from above. This particular Supreme Being had made the rounds of all the tribes, finally reaching the Gros Ventres, and when they discovered that he ate and slept like they did, they knew he wasn't the Supreme Being. It was disappointing.

The Supreme Being was very important and was always the first to be invited to a sweat lodge.

Jim was curious about how he was received when he was so sick. He asked, "Maggie, please tell me about my ailment."

"Jim," she said, "we have two kinds of illnesses. Some are

ascribed to natural causes. The others are supernaturally caused. The difference is not always clear.

"You had tuberculosis, with which many have a soul-loss. The soul is not inside the body or any organ, but is near or around the body. When you were brought to our camp, as you got worse your soul grew farther and farther away from your body. If it had gone too far, you would have died. When you were taken to the sweat lodge, we all prayed to bring your soul closer to your body. The medicine we gave you, which you were never told about, was raw liver and blood from a freshly killed buffalo."

"Thank you, Maggie, for not telling me until now. But it seemed to cure me," Jim said with a smile. "You also gave me a lot of that good tea."

"The sage bush is used for many cures. You only take the small, tender top leaves."

"I'm sorry, Maggie, if I ask so many questions. But I want to learn and I see so much going on around me."

"I have some books, if you would like to read them. The people in the village make fun of me because I read. It is also why I'm getting old and no one wants me for a wife."

"You are the most beautiful woman I have ever seen, and you should be proud that you have schooling," Jim said.

Maggie beamed.

Jim knew that the winter camp broke up in April, when the buffalo started to move.

The Gros Ventres had three seasonal rites, held in the spring, fall and winter. It was during the spring rite that the various bands which had scattered during the winter gathered again at a designated place for a buffalo hunt. The world would be waking up again. Trees would be in leaf, grass growing everywhere, the sage in bloom. The Gros Ventres would pray to the Supreme Being that there would be plenty of game and plant foods, that the people would have an abundance of all things they needed during the year, that there would be no sickness, and that all would live happily.

The days started to go too fast for Jim, and he couldn't get enough time with Maggie. His knowledge of the tribe grew and he was accepted by them.

As spring came, all were warned to stay off the ice and on high ground. The warm Chinook winds were blowing and as Jim and the tribe looked out over the Missouri, the black water started to flow both under and above the ice, lifting huge sections and standing them on their ends. Then the ice broke and the river rose, and the big hunks of ice picked up momentum on the flowing water and collided in tremendous bangs. It was explained to Jim that the ice upriver jammed into a gorge and formed a dam, and when this jam broke, a flood poured down the Missouri, tearing at the banks and even altering the course of the river. For days this went on.

Jim spent hours on a hill, watching this mass of water, ice, mud and debris. The frozen surface swelled and cracked and split into thousands of pieces, and more ice from upriver surged over the top every day. Jim could see, mixed in with the black water and ice, tree limbs and roots which had been ripped from the river banks as the ice carved its way through the earth.

More and more excitement moved through the village as the tribe members prepared for spring.

It was almost time for Jim to be on his way.

Maggie gave him a language lesson one afternoon; Jim asked her to walk to where they could see the river. When they reached the bluff they saw the river running wild. Jim asked Maggie to sit down.

"Maggie," he started, "I have been with you for almost four months. You have become very special to me. I know I'm older than you, I'm white — hell, Maggie, I'm in love with you. I want you to be my wife."

"Jim, I love you also, but figured you would be gone come spring."

"Maggie, I want you to be part of my life."

Jim took Maggie in his arms and kissed her for the first time. "You have made me so happy."

Maggie took Jim's hand as they started back to camp. "I'm very happy also."

The afternoon went slowly for Jim. He couldn't seem to catch Horse Capture alone. Finally he walked right up to him. He said, "Capture, I need to talk to you. It's important to me. I'd like it to be in private — please."

A wide smile spread across Capture's face. He said, "Let's take a walk now, before our evening meal."

They walked a short way from camp. Jim just went ahead and said it. "I love your daughter and want to marry her, Horse Capture. I will pay you anything. I just want to be with her."

"I knew why you wanted to talk to me. I thought you would ask sooner or later," said Capture.

"It will be complicated, and you have to trust me," Jim broke in. "We will have an arranged wedding with you and also a Christian marriage. I will need to borrow a horse to get back to Fort Benton to gather supplies and whatever else you want. I'll have to find a priest too. I promise I'll be good to her, and no one will be disrespectful to her."

"Jim, it will be very hard for you, Maggie and your children. But I know you will be good to her and she will be a good wife. You have my permission."

Jim grabbed the Chief's hand and shook it; the two men smiled.

Over the next week, Jim and Capture worked out what Capture wanted and what Jim would have to buy in Fort Benton. The final arrangement was five horses, two trading post blankets, some sugar and a new rifle with ammunition.

Maggie still wasn't sure Jim would really come back. But he kept telling her that nothing would stop him.

Jim was preparing to leave when word came that buffalo had been seen, moving north. Jim went up on the hill and as far as he could see, a black blanket covered the earth. The buffalo were marching right into the Missouri River, and those in the rear were impatient for those in front to swim out of the way. But when the front line reached the other side they found themselves facing a cliff, and unless they scrambled out of the way, they were trampled by the others reaching the shore from behind. And of those, many only made it halfway up and would then flounder and fall back into the water.

The buffalo continued in the nearly impossible task of making a trail up the steep cliff. Hundreds of the weaker animals died in the struggle and their bodies collected all along the river banks. Other weakened buffalo would make it to the top of the cliff, only to die later.

Jim couldn't believe what he was seeing, the great sacrifice of nature.

After the buffalo passed, the camp started to break up. Jim found out the area where the summer camp would be, said all his goodbyes, held Maggie close to him and told her he would be back as soon as possible.

The trip back only took Jim six days — he pushed his horse, no, Capture's — a little hard.

CHAPTER FIVE

Jim's Return

ARRIVING IN FORT BENTON, the first place Jim headed was Perkins' restaurant.

"Perkins, you know where I might find my brother?"

Perkins walked over to Jim and gave him a big bear hug. "Sure do, Jim. Good to see you alive. John's over at the hotel; was going to leave in the next couple of days to find you. Sure like your buckskins. You look like a mountain man."

"I'll be back for dinner, Perkins. I missed your cooking."

Jim headed for the hotel and found John's room. When John opened the door he said, "Damn! Give me heart failure!" and hugged his brother. "You look good! What'd you do all winter?"

Jim was just as relieved to see that John had made it. "The Gros Ventres treated me like one of the family. Guess I was sick a long time. Still have a cough. But I learned the language and I'm on good terms — even borrowed back my own horse."

John laughed. "Sorry 'bout that, Jim, but I had to give them something. It's been such a hard winter — never knew whether you made it. We did good on the hides. Still got the wagon and team. Sit down and tell me everything."

Jim wasn't sure how to break the news to him, but he had always felt like he could say anything to John. "Biggest thing I have to tell you is — are you ready? I'm going to marry a girl named Maggie who's a full-blood Gros Ventre. Close your mouth; I'm probably going to have more surprises for you."

"None will be as big a surprise as that. When's all this going to happen?"

"As soon as I get the supplies together and find a job. Hope to get a trading post so I can trade with the Gros Ventres. I want to go over to the American Fur Company tomorrow."

John laughed again. "Guess I'm to blame for this one. Well, I hope you don't want me to spend another winter up here. It's just too cold for me."

"John, I want you to stay up here and be my partner."

"That's going to take some thought. I'll help you through this marriage and finding a job at least. In the meantime, let's go get some food."

Jim knew better than to push his brother. He was slow at taking to new things, always had been.

"Good to see you brothers back together," smiled Perkins, seeing them enter the restaurant. "Sure tired of listening to John worrying all winter. You want a couple of the specials?"

"Yes, please, and also lots of hot coffee. Haven't had that in a long time," Jim said.

"Coming right up."

"Jim has a lot of news to tell. He's going to marry an Indian woman."

"Is that true, Jim?"

"It is, Perkins. She's a Gros Ventre. Worked here at Fort Benton for an army officer named Walsh who moved out last spring."

"I know her — her white name's Maggie Walsh. Great lady, very smart and beautiful. Many whites wanted to marry her. Wouldn't give them the time of day. You're a lucky man, Jim."

"Thank you, Mr. Perkins. Now I gotta find five good horses — her father wants them. And she wants to be married by a priest. Got to find one of those too. Then I want a job at one of the trading posts."

"I'll help you any way I can," Perkins said. "I think the Northwest Fur Company needs an agency at the Musselshell post. No spot for a timid soul, called Fort Hawley. But you need to speak the language of the Blackfeet."

"I learned it while I was sick. I'll talk to them tomorrow. It's worth the try."

"Horses should be easy enough," John said. "People who left on the boats last fall sold them off cheap. You know, I have over three thousand of your dollars from the hides. We can stop at the stables on the way to the fur company and see what kind of selection they have in horses."

Jim smiled gratefully at his brother, and the next morning, they went.

"Pete, what do you got in the way of horses for sale? Going to need about six, one with a good saddle and some gear."

"I got a whole pen out back. Your choice. A hundred twenty-five each, and I'll give you your choice of saddle out of that pile over in the corner."

"These look like good horses," John said. "You pick out the ones you want. He'll probably take six hundred fifty."

Jim and John picked through the twenty-five or so horses. All were well taken care of and had good shoes.

At last Jim walked back inside and said, "I'll take those horses I cut out in the side corral, and a good saddle, and give you six-fifty in cash. I want you to brand them with the letters 'J.W.' — make it look like this." Jim drew a picture of how he wanted the brand to look. "So no one'll think they're stolen. We got a deal?"

"It's a deal," Pete said as he shook Jim's hand.

"I want you to make a bill of sale for all six to 'Horse Capture.' Also want you to put some brands on my horse. I got horses — now I need a job."

When they entered the Northwest Fur Company building, Jim asked for Mr. Hawley. A short, stocky man came out to greet the brothers and invited them into his office. "The clerk said you wanted a job, Mr. Wells. Said you have trading experience."

"Yes," Jim said. "I worked at our family trading post until I was twenty years old. Then worked for Wells Fargo in San Francisco for nearly five years. And I spent the winter with the Gros Ventres so I speak the language."

Mr. Hawley said, "I have a post at Fort Hawley; there's a man there named George Boyd. Wants to leave. I'd need you right away because some boats will be coming upriver and trading will start soon. But it's a tough post. We lost woodchoppers and some of the traders to hostiles. You'd need to work with us about a week on how we do things and then we'll figure your pay."

"I want the job," answered Jim. "I'm getting married on the way, and I'll take my wife down with me. I could start tomorrow."

"It's a deal, Jim. Will start you tomorrow. Also might use your experience on the Pony Express and Wells Fargo. We're talking about a North Overland Pony Express from Minnesota through Fort Hawley."

"Thanks a lot, Mr. Hawley. Got my horses, found a job, now have to dig up a priest somewhere."

Jim was to learn that Fort Hawley was a small fort, although the company wanted to expand it. At present it had a single post building with living quarters in the back and a couple of outbuildings.

He had seen many posts and had some time now to think about what he would need. To start, the required list of items might be: blankets of various kinds, cloth, tin kettles, fancy bridles, showy buttons, axes, scalping knives, beads, files, shells, hatchets, wide leather belts, and foodstuffs such as flour, sugar, salt, pepper, coffee, tobacco, and liquor.

As for the liquor, Jim knew about the secret recipe used by other traders. Missouri River water, alcohol, strychnine, tobacco, soap, red pepper, and sagebrush all went into the mixture and was boiled until it turned brown. One bottle of the stuff traded for one buffalo robe. Many traders got rich on this recipe but Jim wasn't interested in making anyone sick or cheating them.

In the week ahead, Hawley primed Jim on the post. The bargaining with both whites and Indians would be up to him, one case at a time, and goods traded would vary with the number of furs offered. Jim was told that the Indians loved to linger over their bargaining, and the more fun they had while they haggled, the less they would be willing to take for their robes.

An Indian squaw could usually prepare no more than ten buffalo robes a year, so a man with more than one wife could produce more robes for trading. Robes would vary in value from one dollar to five on the average. Jim was to learn that the scraping and tanning of the robes was a slow, hard job. The robes were usually made from the buffalo cows. The Indians could be very careless and often several cows would be killed to make only one robe. The bulls were killed for their tongues, humps, and hides, to make thongs and tipi covers.

Jim knew he must learn the difference in robes, with even higher prices paid for especially fine hides. Beaver skins were worth about two dollars. The red fox brought about one dollar, a large wolf hide usually brought one dollar, and ordinary gray foxes and wolves were usually valued at twenty-five to thirty-five cents. And once again the value of the buffalo tongue was brought to Jim's attention. It was used by the Indians and the whites on the plains, and now from the east coast came a steady demand for this prized meat.

Since salt, sugar and coffee were priced at about one dollar a pint, flour at about twenty-five cents a pint, a common formula for trade might be: ten cups of sugar buy one robe, ten robes make up one pony, two ponies make one tipi.

Other traders often gave the Indians quantity rather than quality, knowing that an assortment of interesting trinkets would please them.

The most harmful article of trade was, of course, whiskey. The U.S. Government made attempts to prevent liquor from reaching the Indians, but with the profits so high for the traders, the task became hopeless. And sadly, the Indians had acquired an appetite for it.

As Jim received more training, he vowed to be fair with the Indians.

Hawley informed Jim that his salary would be $1,200 per year, free room and board, and a percentage of profits. John would get $800 per year, board and room, and a percentage of the profits also.

By the end of the week, Jim was ready. His whole life was ahead of him, as wide open and promising as the land itself. He couldn't help smiling when he thought about how surprised Maggie would be to see him again so soon.

CHAPTER SIX

The Marriage

JOHN WONDERED HOW JIM would ever find the Gros Ventres in this wide open space. Jim seemed to smell the direction.

Traveling with them was Father Giorda, a Jesuit. The first night in camp, Jim asked him about the Jesuits and how they ended up in Montana.

Father Giorda told him, "The first in the territory was Father DeSmet. He arrived in eighteen-forty, and was given the name 'Black Robe' by the tribes he encountered. He was soon overwhelmed by the size of this area and returned to St. Louis to find other brothers to return with him."

"Father," Jim said, "I'm a Protestant Christian. You are the first Catholic priest I've ever been around."

"As you can see, we are all the same: me, you, the Indians all believe in the one God or Great Spirit." Father Giorda smiled. "I will tell why I'm here. It was in the late winter of sixty-two, and I was staying at St. Peter's Mission. It was the first break in the weather and I wanted to take in the lay of the land. I foolishly wandered down to the Missouri and began to walk out on the ice. Just as you might expect, I suddenly felt it give way. I instinctively extended my arms so that I would sink no lower than my armpits, but was very frightened, clinging to the ice with my hands, my feet carried up under the surface of the ice by the rapid current. Would the ice break away? My lower body had lost all feeling from the cold, and I shouted for help. Would it ever come? Two brothers from the mission heard my cry and an Indian who had pitched his tipi near the new mission hurried over carrying a lariat. While the brothers stood gaping, the Indian cast me the rope and dragged me to safety. I realized that after God, I owed my life to this Indian. I vowed to devote the rest of my life to working with the Indians of this territory. Now I need my rest and it is going to be at least six days before you find your tribe, so goodnight and bless you."

Jim and John sat by the campfire, watching the flames. They could hear Father Giorda snoring over by the wagon.

"It's something to think about these priests out here, with no family or wife, just working with the Indians," Jim said. "This Father Giorda's quite a guy."

After a breakfast of coffee and hard biscuits, the three set out on their second day of trying to find the Gros Ventre camp. They started to see game: antelope, deer and large herds of buffalo. John was able to shoot a small antelope. The hide was salted and rolled up: they would give it to someone at the Indian camp. That night they had antelope stew with potatoes, carrots, fresh coffee and biscuits. The weather was still cool enough that the remaining meat wouldn't spoil. In fact, it tasted much better after aging a couple of days.

By the third day out they had settled into their routine and were covering about twenty-five miles a day.

John liked to ride on his horse, checking out the trail. This left Jim and Father Giorda in the wagon. But they did like talking during the day, with all that bouncing.

Father Giorda was expensive — $150 and a horse to get back with. But that's what Jim had offered and he wanted everything to be perfect.

That evening Father Giorda said he wanted to hear about Jim and John, so they told him how they had come from Indiana to San Francisco and finally to Montana, and how Jim had become sick and was now making a commitment to stay in Montana. John still hadn't decided about that.

The fifth day out, they ran into a rainstorm which made the going slower. By evening it was clear but cold. Father Giorda wanted to fix the evening meal; he proved to be a good cook. He fried steaks from the antelopes with potatoes. They had biscuits with honey that he had brought, and boiled coffee. He put an eggshell in the coffee which made the grounds settle, so they had their first cups of coffee on the trail without grounds.

"Come on, Father, tell us more of your stories," John said.

"All right. In February of sixty-two, I started out from St. Peter's with a guide, my destination being the Gros Ventre winter camp somewhere north of Fort Benton. On the way, another band of Gros Ventres captured us. During the night my guide escaped, but the marauders took my horse and everything I had; and as if that weren't enough, they stripped me of the clothes on my back, even my undergarments. One of the war party immediately put on my red flannel undershirt, and kindly offered his own costume, a vermin-infested hide of some kind, in exchange. I later learned that the temperature that day was well below zero, and I am amazed that I did not perish.

"Somehow I made my way to the Chief, who handed me a

buffalo skin for a covering. He could hardly believe that I was a Black Robe. Not long after, my things were returned to me. In spite of such unexpected humiliations, I baptized one hundred thirty-four children of the tribe. I was pleased. So you see, I do know the Gros Ventres. I have been back many times since."

"I'll be damned — you know the Gros Ventres and were coming out here anyway," said Jim.

"If you did a little checking you would have found this out, Jim."

"Well your next visit is coming up the next day or so, and I'll make sure you don't lose your clothes again," laughed Jim.

On the evening of the sixth day, they sighted the camp of the Gros Ventres. The women and children ran out to welcome the wagon.

"I see you made an impression on these people when you were here," Father Giorda said. "It looks like you are coming home."

Jim was overwhelmed by the sea of people rushing to greet him. "I see Maggie," he said joyfully. He stopped the wagon and jumped down just in time to catch her in his arms. "I told you I'd be back. And with a priest."

Maggie had tears in her eyes as she hugged and kissed him. At last she turned and saw Father Giorda.

"Father!" said Maggie. "I haven't seen you in a long time. Jim, how did you get him to come out here?"

"At gunpoint. Where is your lodge? And your father?"

"He is waiting for you."

"Come, Maggie, I'll put you up on the wagon."

He lifted her up so she could get on the bench and headed the wagon in the direction of one of the larger tipis.

"Maggie, I'm so happy to see you. I've been lonesome without you."

Maggie put her arm under his and smiled up at him. What

a feeling it gave him. He was very much in love with her, and seeing her again made that feeling even stronger.

Horse Capture emerged from his tipi to greet them. "Jim," he said, "I see you are a man of your word. You have brought my horse back; you have taken good care of him. And here is your brother John — I didn't know him without all that hair on his face. And the Black Robe Father Giorda. Father is very famous with us. He came to us without anything. We will all eat in my lodge tonight. Tomorrow we will all sweat and pray for this union. I will see if what you bring is enough."

Jim said, "I brought you six good horses, food, cloth and a new rifle with lots of ammunition. I would like a feast that all will remember. I want your traditional marriage, and also a marriage performed by Father Giorda. It needs to happen within the next couple of days, since I must go to Fort Hawley to run the trading post."

Horse Capture said, "The marriage can be the day after tomorrow."

Jim took Maggie's hand.

In the morning, a sweat was prepared. Jim, John and Father Giorda were led into the sweat lodge. They had all stripped down and been given a loincloth. There they smoked the sacred pipe, and the medicine man gave a prayer:

> O' Great Spirit, no matter where we look
> In your universe, we see your great wonders.
> Just look at the eagle. Oh you magnificent flyers,
> Who carry the spirit of our grandfathers.
> We have learned to be hunters by your
> Dashing hunting skills.
> You are fast enough to take the grouse and
> Ptarmigan on the wing.
> With your great power and strength,

I have seen you bring down a deer.
Your feathers are sacred to me and are used
To remind us of the power of the Great Spirit.
Your feathers are worn by our chiefs and
Warriors as a sign of power and protection.
Of all the power that is given to us by you, the Great Spirit,
Your symbol through the eagle is very great.
My prayer of thanks to you, Great Spirit,
For this symbol of your power.

During the sweat the medicine man called to the grandfathers and the eagle "to give us all strength and help Jim in his new life."

After four sweats of about ten minutes each, they all left the lodge and went to the river to bathe. Jim and John were presented with new buckskins, Father Giorda with his cassock. Then Jim was invited to Horse Capture's lodge.

Inside the lodge, Maggie was at Capture's side. She was in the most beautiful buckskin dress he had ever seen. It was covered with beadwork and feathers. Her hair was braided with feathers on the ends. He stood there with his mouth open.

"Jim, sit down," Horse Capture said with a smile.

He sat across from Capture but couldn't stop looking at Maggie.

"Jim, a marriage is usually between two families and all arrangements are made before a woman is given to a man. Today I must deal with you directly. You have brought me six horses plus the one you used. This is good. It shows she means a lot to you and you will take care of her. I'm not sure an Indian should marry a white. I have not seen many good marriages. But if you love her and are not ashamed before other whites, you will take care of her."

Jim said, "Capture, I will never be ashamed to be married

to this wonderful woman. I love her and will take care of her as long as I live. I do worry about something happening to me; if that happens, then she can come back to you."

"You have brought many gifts, Jim. I'm a man of wealth and I'm giving you a new tipi with all new robes and other things you will need. You may take Maggie. She is yours."

Jim felt like the luckiest man in the world.

"Capture, as you know, tomorrow we will be married by a priest. Maggie may go to our new tipi and I will go tomorrow. I would also like to offer the people food for a feast tomorrow, so your whole tribe can celebrate with us."

"You might change our tradition. The marriage was validated when you presented the gifts to me."

"I know, but this is what Maggie wishes, and I want everything to be perfect for her."

"Jim, you are making a mistake letting a woman tell you what to do. Especially Maggie."

All during their conversation, Maggie was not able to say a word, but she could see how much Jim loved her and respected her wishes. She would sleep alone for the last time in the new tipi. Tomorrow Jim would join her.

Jim took Maggie's hand and led her out of the lodge. All the women were standing there smiling and laughing, waiting for the newlyweds to go to the new tipi. A great shock went through the camp as Jim took Maggie to the entrance, gave her a kiss, and walked away.

"Well, Father," Jim said, "I'm a married man and tomorrow I get married again — twice in two days."

Father Giorda said, "You sound a little nervous. It's too late — you're already married. In the eyes of the church the sacrament is between the two of you. I'm only the witness. We shall bless and give you your Christian marriage tomorrow."

"Father, she is a wonderful girl."

Jim and Father Giorda walked over to where John was warming himself by a fire.

"Well, John, you have a married brother and tomorrow we put the final link in the chain."

"I know you both will be happy," John said as he gave his brother a big hug. "Tomorrow she'll be part of our family, a very welcome part."

"Thank you, John. That means a lot to me."

Jim and John woke to a lot of noise. The food Jim brought was cooking and everyone could feel the excitement building.

Only the best part of the buffalo, the hump, tongue and tenderloin, were being prepared for this feast. Jim could see that some puppies had been killed. He knew this was a great delicacy, along with elk, deer and antelope. He saw many vegetables; some he knew, others he didn't, such as turnips and bitterroot.

The wedding was set for mid-morning, which meant that the eating would last the rest of the day.

Father Giorda had set up an altar in the center of the camp. On it was draped a white cloth; two candles and a gold crucifix stood in the middle. Small children brought flowers to the altar.

The people of Maggie's tribe gathered around the altar. John stood at his side, his best man. Father Giorda appeared in vestments that had been beaded by the Indians.

At last Maggie's father brought her out. She was wearing the beautiful beaded buckskin dress she had worn the previous day. Her hair was in long braids studded with eagle feathers.

Her father wore his headdress and looked like a very powerful chief.

Maggie put her arm in Jim's and he could feel her shaking, or was he the one shaking? She was beautiful.

They both turned to Father Giorda, who raised his arms and said, "This is a great day for Jim and Maggie and for all of us who are part of this ceremony." He turned and started the mass. It was all in Latin, and the Indians began singing in beautiful voices.

When Father Giorda was about twenty minutes into the service, he stopped and moved closer to Jim and Maggie. "Are you ready to exchange your vows?"

"We are," said Jim.

"Do you, James, take Margaret for your lawful wife, to have and to hold, in sickness and in health, for richer or poorer, until death do you part?"

"I do."

"I never asked you, Jim — do you have a ring?"

"Yes I do, Father."

"The ring please."

Father Giorda blessed the ring and gave it to Jim. "Put it on her finger and say, 'With this ring I thee wed.'"

"With this ring I thee wed." Jim slipped the gold band on Maggie's finger.

"You are man and wife. You may kiss her."

Jim put his arm around Maggie and gave her a big hug and a kiss. All the crowd started to yell and laugh and cheer.

"Today Jim has pledged his life to Maggie and to the uniting of two people from two different worlds, which will now become one. Let us all pray for the Father, the Great Spirit in the prayer he taught us:

Our Father, O Great Spirit,
Who art in heaven,
Hallowed be thy name;
Thy kingdom come, thy will be done,
On earth as it is in heaven.
Give us this day our daily bread;
And forgive us our trespasses
As we forgive those who trespass against us;
And lead us not into temptation,
But deliver us from evil.

Maggie's people finished the Mass with a song.

Jim, Maggie, John, Father Giorda and Capture sat on buffalo robes in a place of honor. Horse Capture led a prayer to the buffalo:

O' Great Spirit, you have shown me your great power
Through the creatures you have put on Earth.
Your buffalo is your sign of endurance and power.
They are on your plains in abundance for our use.
There is no waste on this great creature.
His hide is for warmth and protection. This warmth is your
Way of showing your affection and kindliness.
His tendons are used for our bow strings, so we are
Able to get other game.
His bladder can be used for a water bottle,
Or for a game of sport.
His meat can be used for a feast or
Dried for use on trips or in the winter.
His horns and bones become utensils and tools for use
Around the lodge, and his ribs have ever been used
By the spirits for a bow.
O' Great Spirit, you have shown us your great power

By giving us this creature.
Let us always cherish your great gift, and let us not abuse
Your gift.

At the end of the prayer, the medicine man went around and took samples of all the food, put it in a bowl, and carried it to a mound near the sweat lodge which had a buffalo skull on it. He put the bowl in front of the skull and lit some sage. He chanted, passing the smoke all around the mound. When he came back and sat down, the feast began.

Jim asked Father Giorda if he planned to build a mission out in this area. He said at the present time, no. He was still in trouble with his superiors for purchasing an opera house in Virginia City. It was the first Catholic church in Virginia City and he renamed it "All Saints."

Jim had really grown to like this priest during his contact with him.

"With the money from you, I want to do some work on our mission at St. Peter's, which is being hit by raiding parties of northern Blackfeet and other tribes. The mission has been struggling for years."

"Father, are you trying to make me feel guilty and pay more?"

"No, Jim, but you will see what a struggle these missions have, the longer you are out here."

The food started coming and it all tasted wonderful.

"John," Maggie said, "if you see a girl you want but she does not have an eye for you, you can go to the medicine man and he will give you a packet of powder. You take it and keep it in your pocket very safe and do not let anyone see it or touch it. Now you watch this girl, and watch carefully — you do not want to make a mistake. Then when she goes out of the lodge to relieve herself, watch her so you can locate the exact spot.

Then open the little packet and dip in it the tip of a little sliver of wood. Go over to the spot and stick the sliver right into the ground on the spot where she urinated. That is all you have to do. In a short time this girl will come running after you. She will be very anxious and beg you to take her."

"Maggie, you're pulling my leg," John said.

"I told you it worked on Jim."

John laughed and felt closer to Maggie with her sense of humor. He knew they would get along.

"Maggie, it will be hard for you to leave here in a couple of days. Your family, your friends, your life."

"When we marry we are prohibited by law to marry anyone related by blood, no matter how remote the tie. So we know when we marry we will be going to live with another band, and we know this all our lives. We are also given to live with other relatives. I was an exception. Our marriages are arranged between husband-to-be and one of the males in my family. When I was about seven years old, I was sent away from home to my grandmother's lodge to be trained to do women's work. Then when a girl is ten or eleven, she is handed over to a man in marriage. I went to Fort Benton to work for a white family instead. You know, John, an Indian can have more than one wife?"

"Yes, I do, Maggie," he grinned. "But can a wife have more than one husband?"

Maggie laughed at her new brother-in-law.

The party went on all afternoon. They couldn't put their bowls down empty; someone would fill it with another new dish. Jim felt like he couldn't eat another bite and was anxious to be alone with Maggie.

"Maggie, when can we sneak away?"

"As soon as the sun sets."

John was out trying the Indian dances. He was enjoying

himself. Jim hoped he would stay with them and not leave in the fall. But it was his life.

They would stay here two more nights and then must get on the trail for Fort Hawley. At least the wagon was almost empty and Maggie didn't have much to bring. It was also nice getting rid of all those horses.

It was one of the most beautiful sunsets Jim had ever seen. He looked at Maggie and took her hand. "I love you, Maggie."

"I love you too, Jim. Let's go to our lodge."

They started for the lodge, their first home.

When Jim threw back the flap, a small fire was burning in the center. Everything was new and clean. He took Maggie's arm, turned her and picked her up. "It's our tradition to carry the new wife into the home."

When they were inside, he let her down, turned her to him and kissed her. "Jim, please close the flap," she said.

"Yes, I will, fast."

Near the fire was the buffalo robe bed. Jim sat down and pulled Maggie down next to him. "This lodge is nice. Everything is all set up."

"Jim, take your clothes off and get under the robe. I want to get ready to join you."

He took off his clothes and kneeled down on the robes. He could see Maggie taking the beads out of her hair and combing it. Then she took off her dress and stood by the fire naked for a few moments. He could feel his whole body reacting.

She pulled back the robe and pressed close to him. They made love for most of the night.

When Jim woke in the morning, he thought it was all a dream until he looked over and saw Maggie next to him. He leaned over and kissed her on the nose, cheeks and lips. She opened her eyes and smiled. They made love again.

It must have been mid-morning when they finally left the tipi. Maggie wanted to go down to the river and bathe and wanted Jim to go with her. The water was still very cold and he wasn't able to stay in as long as she could.

When they were dressed, food was brought to them in their lodge. After they ate, Maggie told Jim to go and attend to his stock. She wanted to clean the lodge and wash the blood from their bed robes. When she came out of the lodge with the bed robes, all the old ladies stood around, pointing and smiling. She carried the robes with pride.

Jim found John and Father Giorda by the river talking. "You converted my brother yet, Father?" he asked.

"No, but we thought you'd died. It's almost noon and you're just getting up."

"Didn't get much sleep. Too much noise from all that singing, dancing and yelling."

"Wife throw you out already and tell you to go to work? See, life changes fast after marriage."

"Yeah. See you boys. Don't have much to talk about if you only got me. By the way, John, I want to check the team and wagon. Want to pull out of here tomorrow. We still have a long trip ahead of us. You want to come with us, Father?"

"No, I should get back to my mission. But I'll surprise you someday."

In the mid-afternoon, Maggie came out and she and Jim took a walk up on a hill. From the hilltop they could look down on the camp; in one direction, open land for miles; in the other, herds of buffalo. They sat there for a long time, just holding each other in silence. The land was rough and wild, yet calm and beautiful. It was to be their home.

Maggie told Jim that they had a prayer to water that the Great Spirit had given them. It went:

O' Great Spirit, what is the one great thing
That you shower us with and is always a part of all plans?
It is the fluid water.
Water is transparent,
Yet it reflects our image back to us.
Water is used to cleanse both the outer body
And the inner spirit.
You have made great rivers on which our bull boats can
Travel, and small rivers of water criss-cross the land,
Making it easy for us to travel.
The falling water in the spring makes the buffalo grass
Grow tall and green.
The falling water makes the new and special food
Of spring and summer, berries, nuts and plums.
The falling water also brings a new abundance
Of game for fresh meat.
Each thing you give us, O' Great Spirit,
Is so perfect with so many uses.
O' Great Spirit, let us not abuse this great thing
You have given to us.

When Maggie finished, Jim told her how beautiful it was to have prayers like these for all the things the Great Spirit had given them. And a worry nagged at him too. Would he be able to protect her, and everything that she came from?

"Maggie, tomorrow we leave for the new job at Fort Hawley. I'm looking forward to building us a home."

When they got back to camp, Maggie went to prepare dinner for Jim, John and Father Giorda. While she was cooking, John took Jim aside. "Jim, I need to talk to you. I know you're not going to like this, but I've decided I'm heading back to California."

Jim smiled. He already had a feeling life in the Territory wasn't for John. "Don't want to spend another winter freezing?"

"Pretty soft, I guess," John said.

"It's all right," Jim said. "If I hadn't met Maggie, who knows where I'd want to be. But damn! What am I going to do without you, little brother?"

"I feel the same way, Jim, but let's not think about it. All right?"

"Good idea," Jim said.

Jim went down to the stream to wash his face. When he returned his guests had arrived; they all sat down to the meal prepared by Maggie.

Father Giorda told them he was also leaving tomorrow but wanted to keep in touch with them and expected Jim and Maggie to name their first son Joseph after him. He was anxious to get back to St. Mary's, since that was his headquarters. Since he had re-opened the mission in 1866, everything had to be rebuilt. He wanted to see the new altar that Father Ravalli was building.

In the morning everyone was up early. Maggie helped load the wagon and started to take down the tipi. By late morning the wagon was ready to move out of the camp. Horse Capture kissed his daughter goodbye and Maggie sat up on the wagon with Jim; they felt they could make Fort Hawley in about three days.

John rode with them on his horse for a couple of miles; then he gave Jim and Maggie a salute and with the pounding of hooves was again on his way west.

CHAPTER SEVEN

Fort Hawley

FORT HAWLEY WAS SQUEEZED on the edge of a narrow shelf beside the Missouri river beneath a wall of crumbling yellow bluffs. The stockade was full of holes and missing a gate and inside, one old building stood half collapsed. Jim and Maggie were surprised when they reached their destination.

"This place look abandoned to you, Maggie?" Jim said.

"Yes it does."

But as they climbed out of the wagon, some men came out of the ramshackle fort to meet them. "You Jim Wells?" one said.

"I am. And this is my wife Maggie Wells."

"I'm Bill Norris," the tallest man said. "This is Dennis Halpin, Bill Martin, Joe Bushway, and that's Frenchy."

"Got yourself a squaw?" said Dennis.

"Boys, we want to start out as friends," Jim said. "This is my wife and she'll get respect at all times from everyone, understood?"

"Sorry boss, but we just don't see pretty women around here," Dennis apologized.

Jim pulled the wagon into the stockade, unhitched the team and put the horses in the corral. He helped Maggie unload the tipi and they found a place behind the store to put it up. "I guess, Maggie, we'll be living in your tipi until I can put up a cabin." He looked at his beautiful new wife. "I hope you don't let the stupid things these boys say bother you. Once they know you they'll change their minds."

"I knew it would be hard," Maggie said. "Don't worry. I'll set up the lodge and start dinner."

Jim did worry about these affronts to Maggie and the toll they might take. But he also believed that her goodness would prevail over anyone stupid enough to doubt her. Maybe the two of them, in some small way, could help end the hatred that existed between the whites and the Indians.

Jim spent the next hour inspecting the fort. It almost looked like a lost cause. He knew they would have Sioux problems and that they needed to get this place into shape fast. He gathered the men by the broken gate later in the afternoon.

"First, boys, sorry I didn't get here earlier, but I got married on the way. Now we need to work twice as hard. I want everyone to start cutting logs in the morning so we can re-roof the post. I want to build two new cabins and a new store house. This means enlarging the stockade and fixing those gates. In the afternoons some of us will cut cord wood for the boats. The rest will continue building. We can all bring in fresh game. Maggie will cook. Any questions?"

The men were prepared to work hard and appreciated Jim's no-nonsense approach.

That evening they all had their first real meal in some time: roast elk, biscuits and fresh coffee. And for the next several days the constant sound of chopping and hammering could be heard; within the week the trading post was almost repaired, the stockade enlarged, the gates working.

Getting up the bunkhouse would be the next project. Jim and Maggie's house would come last; Jim found he liked tipi living. Maggie was always at his side doing as much work as any of the men, and she had quickly gained their respect.

Indians began to arrive to trade, erecting their tipis along the bottom land and bluffs nearby. The first boat carrying trading supplies was expected any day.

Early one morning, when the men were finishing breakfast, word came in that a group of Arapahos was heading for the post. All the men headed out to close the stockade gates. By noon a couple more woodchoppers had come into the fort. Piecing together the information, Jim figured the fort was surrounded by a war party of about eighteen lodges.

In the early afternoon one of the woodchoppers went out to retrieve his horses, which he had left hobbled in the willows. He never came back.

The Indians stayed around the fort forcing Jim and his men to go out for wood and water heavily armed. Finally, the war party realized they couldn't do much harm against the fort, so after the third day they tired of the siege and left. They took the horses in the willows.

Jim went out and retrieved the body of the woodchopper and buried him near the fort.

This was Jim's first meeting with the Arapahos. On the northern plains, Teton Sioux, Northern Cheyennes, and Northern Arapahos had not, in the past, been as directly provoked by white advances as other tribes. But now all the tribes in the area were distressed by the growing traffic of whites to the Montana mines. Some of the gold seekers were going by steamboat up the Missouri River. Others traveled overland on the Bozeman Trail, which cut through the heart of the Sioux buffalo ranges in the Powder River country.

Where in the past there had been trouble mostly from the Sioux, now it could be almost any tribe.

At last the first steamboat came upstream and unloaded its trading supplies at Fort Hawley; it would pick up furs on its way downriver. With the boat came the first newspapers, giving Jim an update on the Indian wars.

General William Tecumseh Sherman was quoted as saying, "We must act with vindictive earnestness against the Sioux, even to their extermination, men, women, and children." Sherman now commanded all the troops on the Great Plains.

In Denver, a Senator Doolittle from the east had spoken to a large crowd about the need to end costly wars and find another solution to the Indian problem. There seemed only two options: to place the Indians on reservations where they could support themselves, or simply exterminate them. The crowd began to scream, "Exterminate them! Exterminate them!"

Jim read on. Apparently there was tension between east and west over the Indian problem. Easterners reacted with horror to reports of large massacres of Indians by the U.S. Army, though the Indian cause had inspired no changes in the laws. In the West, most people were happy to see the Indians wiped out. There was a proposal to put the Indian Bureau back in the War Department, which made sense to many in the West. But the idea offended Easterners and was opposed by the Department of the Interior.

The newspaper went on to say:

The reservation system offered the only hope. The Indians could be civilized and taught to farm. The Military would not do well at such a task, and therefore the Indian Bureau should remain in the Interior Department.

Jim read all this with uneasiness.

"Maggie, how do you feel about the idea of reservations?"

"It is like if I asked you, Jim, how you would feel if your family were placed for the rest of their lives in a prison. Even if for their own protection."

"Maggie, your family *is* my family now," he said, his throat clenching with sorrow.

Spring was upon them and the steamboats arrived, bringing fresh supplies for the storerooms. Parties of Oglala, Yankton, and Santee Sioux were at Fort Hawley to trade, as well as Gros Ventres and Crows from the west and Assiniboines from the north. The settlements of Indians there to trade formed a band of protection around the fort against war parties.

Maggie became the best trader and was allowed full run of the trading post. She conducted the exchange through a shoulder-high "trading hole." The Indians were admitted only a few at a time. The buffalo robe was almost always at the center of the transaction. Jim noticed that the Indians wouldn't divide up the value of a robe; to take half its value in sugar, for example; another half, in coffee. Instead, the Indian usually offered one robe or more for one kind of good only. Three robes bought a Mackinaw blanket; it took many more than that to buy a rifle. Maggie would measure out the staples in tin cups, and often pour them, by instruction, into a corner of the woman's buckskin dress.

The Indian women loved to trade for beads, especially blue ones, and they were fussy picking them out; any that were slightly off were rejected.

Maggie knew that once the trading was over with, the Indians expected some kind of gift, in proportion to the amount of the purchases. For this, Maggie often offered extra beads or trinkets. She and Jim tried to keep the relationship between the whites and the Indians as peaceful as possible. Occasionally someone lost his temper, but usually it passed.

"Sometimes they ask me what I'm doing, working for whites," Maggie told Jim.

"And what do you say?"

"I say I am an Indian first, but my husband is a fair trader, and it is good to see fair trade keep on."

Flour and oatmeal were twenty-five cents a pound. Bacon sold at eighty cents; salt and sugar, from thirty-five cents to a dollar; coffee, never less than sixty cents a pound and frequently at a dollar. A rifle could go for well over one hundred dollars. Prices for tobacco and whiskey varied, according to the supply. When it was scarce, whiskey went for up to a dollar a drink. But when it arrived on the steamboats, the price dropped by half.

One day Jim received a message to attend a meeting the last week in June at Fort Carroll. The fort was about a day's ride upriver; he hated to leave when activity at his own post was at its height. But he went anyway.

Joe Bushway had come from Fort Peck, Allen Bradbury from Fort Benton.

The meeting was to let the trading posts know that the Postmaster General was preparing a contract for mail delivery by Pony Express over what was known as the Northern Overland Trail, from Minnesota to the Montana Territory.

Jim was called upon for assistance because of his former experience with the Pony Express in California. Joe Bushway was to transfer two of his men, Henry MacDonald and Bill Bent, to make up the team working out of Fort Hawley.

Jim agreed to help in any way he could and left early the next morning to be back home by sundown.

The first courier charged out of the Milk River stockade in mid-July. Riders from Fort Union dashed in to Fort Hawley, where another rider was already mounted and waiting. Jim watched the swapping of the mail bags, glad he was doing something a little less frantic now. But it wasn't long before the Northern Overland Pony Express started to have trouble from the Sioux and Assiniboines. A rider might show up at Fort Hawley without his horse, and with gunshot wounds or arrows in his body. Word would come in that one of the stations had burnt down and all men and horses had vanished. Sometimes a rider simply never arrived. But the Pony Express, with all its hazards, went on.

Back in July, Joe Bushway tried to send Bent and MacDonald down to Fort Hawley. The two men asked about Jim Wells and what Bushway's impression of him was. They later told Jim that he had said: "Wells is a man of first-class business ability; he turned Fort Hawley around. He's married to an Indian woman. He is one tough, rough man." MacDonald and Bent had finally made up their minds to give it a try, and showed up at Fort Hawley.

When they walked into the fort, Jim greeted them. "I'm Jim Wells, the local agent. You boys look pretty bad. Let one of us here take your horses; you get inside."

"I'm Henry MacDonald and this here is Bill Bent. We're your new riders."

"Looks like you could use some food."

"We sure can. Only thing we've had lately was an old, scabby, blind buffalo," MacDonald said.

"Don't forget the rosehips," Bent laughed.

"Maggie, can we get these people something to eat? Maggie, my wife, damn good cook. Boys all getting fat around the fort."

Henry MacDonald was impressed by Jim Wells and he knew from that first handclasp that they were to have a lasting friendship.

The food came; it was delicious and there was plenty of it.

They were surprised to see that Maggie was an Indian, but they were quickly impressed by her charm and devotion to Jim.

That night Henry MacDonald explained that everyone called him 'Little Mac" to distinguish him from all the other Scotchmen around, and because he was so young. He told them he was known by all the Indian tribes as "Cut Lip," but was to find that "Little Mac" would stick with him.

MacDonald remembered coming upriver and meeting Father DeSmet, who asked him what had happened to his mouth. With embarrassment, he reached up and placed his hand over his mouth to hide it. But the priest gave him some interesting advice. He told Little Mac that the Indians respected and feared mouths that were unusual, and that his cut lips might save his life.

Mac told Jim and Maggie how he had gotten his "cut lip." He had been a Union soldier until his company ran into a Confederate troop near Petersburg, Virginia. He woke up in a field hospital and was later sent to Lincoln Army General Hospital in Washington. He had suffered a severe mouth and jaw injury and a lacerated right hand. The scars had not faded much at all.

Jim and Maggie enjoyed their first evening with Little Mac. "You boys rest a couple of days before you start to ride. Get settled in the bunkhouse," Jim said, giving each a pat on the back.

The next day Maggie gave each of the new riders a medicine bag to wear around his neck. She would not tell the men what was in their medicine bags.

The new mail route was shorter but no safer from Indian attack. And the attacks now seemed to be for entertainment purposes, for once the Indians discovered that the purpose of all that frantic horse riding was the exchange of a small sack filled with pieces of paper, they deemed the Pony Express a joke. Rather than harm the mail carrier, they might surround him and whoop, rip open his sack and scatter his mail, then take his horse, leaving him to walk with the empty mail bag as all he had to show for himself.

The following week Little Mac rode in with his own story. On his way back to the Fort, carrying his mail bag, he had heard the thundering of distant hooves, and looking off in the distance, realized that a band of Indians was galloping toward him. Mac tightened his saddle and prepared to take off. But he was in a tight place, with mountains behind him, and Beaver Creek, full of beaver dams, impassable before him.

He had to ride back a mile before he found a place to cross. And the Indians altered their course to gain on him. Finally the Indians cornered Little Mac, but when they saw what he was carrying, they simply shouted and circled and laughed, then were on their way.

Little Mac, with his four sacks of mail, reached Hawley safely, but scared. "I kept rubbing my medicine bag from you, Maggie," he said.

In early fall, Jim contracted with a couple of men to put up winter hay for the livestock at Fort Hawley. The hay was to be cut some distance from the fort. The two men left with supplies for ten days.

When Jim had not heard from them in almost two weeks he started to worry. He gathered a few of his men and they traveled up the river to where the cutters had been working. "Hey Jim," one of the boys shouted, "I found the camp. Looks like it's been raided but no sign of the men."

"Let's spread out," Jim said. "Check all the river points for signs."

"Why the points?" one of the men asked.

"The river points are bottoms formed by the bends in the

river. And as you will see, the bottom is usually fringed by a large sand bar. See that one over there? That's a river point," Jim pointed one out to the men. "Easy to find a man's trail. Let's spread out."

It was only a short time before Jim made the discovery he had feared. He felt heartsick remembering the affable men and their gratitude at being hired. "Over here — I've found it." Everyone ran over to the sand bar, and there on the smooth, shiny sand was the trail, showing that a man had been crawling on his hands and knees. "Come on. Let's get moving," Jim beckoned the others.

The trail was a horrible map of the man's last hours, showing how he had crawled hands and knees to the water's edge to drink, then around and around in circles on the sandy beach. Following the blood they found the naked body behind a clump of brush.

"Be careful — they might still be around here. And we don't have much cover," Jim gestured to the men.

The man they found had been stripped, struck on the head with a hatchet, scalped and castrated. How this mutilated person had wandered on his hands and knees so extensively was a horrible thing to imagine.

The sun was bright and they spent the rest of the day with no luck. "I got a feeling we're being watched," one of the men said to Jim.

"Let's get that body back to the fort. Don't want to be out here after dark. They probably took the other man with them." Right as Jim started back to the body a shot rang out, hitting the ground in front of Jim's horse.

"Get down behind that bank! They're up on that bluff!" shouted Jim. "Watch the bluff and only fire if you get a clean shot."

Just then, Jim saw an Indian move near the bluff, take

careful aim and fire. He could see the Indian rise; a shot rang
out from below and the man toppled from the bluff.

"Good aim," Jim said.

They waited for about half an hour but didn't see any
further movement. "Must have been a loner. Let's get out of
here."

"Sure bet, Jim. We're ready to ride."

When they arrived back at the Fort they buried the hay
cutter and paid their respects.

Jim was certain that the Sioux were responsible. And
finally, after numerous episodes of this type, the Postmaster
General called off the Northern Overland Pony Express as of
March 30, 1868 and closed its affairs at Fort Hawley. Jim and
Maggie, with Pomp Dennis, Bill Martin, another man known as
"Seven Up," and Little Mac, prepared to close down the Fort.

But during their final week at Fort Hawley, three men
went up the river from Fort Hawley on horseback to hunt.
Coming back they were waylaid by a party of Assiniboines.
One was injured under his horse. Jim received word about the
situation and with some Gros Ventres went out to assist the men.
Jim was able to come up behind the Assiniboines and kill two;
the rest ran from the area. All the men at the fort, whites and
Indians alike, went to see the dead Assiniboines. The Gros
Ventres emptied their revolvers into them, scalped one, and
left the naked, dead bodies for the wolves.

Many years later, writing about Jim for *The River Press* in
Fort Benton, Little Mac would describe the scalp dance the Gros
Ventres held for Jim the following evening at the fort:

The Indians thought a great deal of Wells — Jim as they
called him. The scalp was placed on a pole and held aloft
over; outside the circle old men sat on the ground and beat
time on the monotonous tom-tom. The singing commenced

with a low, guttural bass, "Hai-ah, hai-ah, hai-ah,"
gradually deepening and rising into a tenor, then with the
shrillest women's voices, rising into a weird soprano shriek;
gradually lessening back to tenor and bass, until it died
away in a sobbing gutteral — then a full assembled war
whoop with a refrain of "Jim, batz, zatz!" (Gros Ventre for
good and strong.) This song was accompanied by a rising and
falling on the toes, with the knees slightly bent, the whole
party making a circular movement. As their blood warmed
and their enthusiasm deepened, the tom-tom beat louder
and louder, the bass was deeper and hoarser, and the
wailing crescendo rose to an unearthly shriek. The bucks
commenced to mimic the motions of war, robes were thrown
of, the rocking motion became a leap, the circle swaying
faster and faster. One old lady, whose only attire consisted
of a robe and who held in her clenched hand a gleaming
knife, sang "Jim, batz-zatz" in the frenzy, threw off the
robe, and continued the dance, which was now a leaping
Pandemonium, as naked as when she was born.

CHAPTER EIGHT

The Musselshell

JIM CLOSED DOWN THE TRADING POST at Fort Hawley. He and Maggie loaded the wagon with all their possessions and headed back for Fort Benton.

On the way they stopped for a couple of days with the Gros Ventres. Horse Capture greeted Jim by his new name. "Welcome, Big and Strong. You now have a Gros Ventre name and are in our songs. Welcome home, Maggie."

"It's good to be home again," Maggie said, reaching out to embrace her father.

Jim said, "They closed down Hawley, but there's talk of a new post at the Musselshell."

The Gros Ventre camp didn't look as prosperous to Jim as it once had; he knew it was because of the killing of the buffalo. Now the Union Pacific Railroad had divided the buffalo into two great herds, northern and southern. The Gros Ventres were having trouble locating any large herds.

It was a relaxing visit. Jim always felt happy

around the Gros Ventres. He didn't want their way of life to change.

When Jim and Maggie arrived in Fort Benton they took a room at the hotel. The manager didn't want Maggie there, but Jim told him she was his wife and they had better change the rules or he would change the place. The manager grumbled and backed down. After they washed up, they went to Perkins' and were greeted with a warm welcome and a great meal.

The next morning Jim headed over to the office. Bradbury greeted Jim and began the meeting.

"You're going to hear angry talk here in Fort Benton about this steamboat port at Musselshell, not to mention the proposed freight wagon road connecting Helena with the Missouri River," Bradbury told him. "But we already have the stockade done and new buildings for storehouses. We also have several cabins built and men busy cutting and hauling logs for more."

"The last time I was there," Jim said, "there were just a few huts on the bluff. They tried this before and called the place Kerchival. What became of it?"

"Kerchival was an experiment, and a bad one at that," Bradbury said. "The Montana Hide and Fur Company, to bring life to the idea again, will have a warehouse, a trading post, wagons waiting for freight, and even a nice town ready when the steamboats begin coming. The plan is for you, Jim Wells, to build an independent stockade on the Missouri. Your partners will be me and T.C. Power. The wagons will follow the route of the Pony Express as far as Judith Butte. From there they'll swing east and go through Crooked Creek Gulch to the Musselshell. We feel that in a few more months, it will be a full stockade and trading post."

"What about the Indian problem? Been cutting a lot of settlements to shreds and stealing a lot of stock," Jim stated.

"To keep the Indians under control, we're making arrangements for troops from the 13th Infantry at Camp Cook at the mouth of the Judith to build a stockade below the town. You know how the Missouri flows — south to north through the Badlands, then turns east to west. But at Musselshell it starts north again before going south at Fort Benton. Frankly, the river looks like a wobbly outline of a breast. Take this section of the Missouri River above the mouth of the Musselshell. At the bottom would be Fort Musselshell, with Fort Benton halfway to Helena. We all know that the right-hand section of the river is full of sand bars and islands and rapids. There are only two months of the year, during high water, when any of the steamboats can get up here to Fort Benton. And we all know that the river is so unnavigable that nothing can pass above Fort Benton because of the islands and the great high falls on the Missouri. We know there are islands below the Musselshell, but nothing like those between there and Benton. Boats will be able to dock at Musselshell a whole month earlier in the spring, a month later in the fall.

"We thought of a port lower down the river, but there's no place to put a port in the badlands.

"So if you draw a line from the Musselshell to Helena, you have your wagon road. This wagon road will avoid all the obstructions in the river and will bring freight directly to Helena for distribution throughout the territory."

"I get it," Jim said.

"You ready to give it a try?"

"I am."

Jim and Maggie celebrated that evening by having another big dinner with Perkins.

Plans were quickly made for Jim and Maggie to move down to the Musselshell to take charge of the new trading post. They were given a choice to go down by boat or by land. They chose the trip overland because they could stay with the Gros Ventres again. The help were already at the Musselshell: Bill Norris, Dennis Halpin and Bill Martin.

Jim and Maggie left Fort Benton again. The trail had become familiar. The weather was holding, thawing during the day but freezing at night. All the creeks and rivers were running full, bank to bank, from the melting snow. The prairie was lush with new prairie grass, which furnished feed for the horses when they were hobbled at night.

They made their camp the first night some twenty miles north and east of Fort Benton. It had been a good drive for the first day out. They found a clear running creek to camp by, and gathered buffalo chips and wood for the campfire. Maggie used a Dutch oven to cook the evening meal. After the meal, Jim took the Dutch oven down to the creek and scrubbed the pot clean with sand. Back at the camp, Maggie had the bed all set up.

"Ouch!" Jim said, climbing in. "What's that?"

Maggie laughed. "Don't you know about heating the bed that way?"

Maggie had gathered a half-dozen medium-sized prairie stones, which she placed in the campfire. Once they were hot, she wrapped them in feed sacks and put them in the buffalo robe bed.

"Get in quick, Jim. I'm right after you."

"Feels pretty good."

The next morning they woke up to rain, which meant slogging through mud and swollen creeks. Jim was anxious to get started, so he hitched up the team and they had a breakfast of cold biscuits and dried meat on the trail.

The rain was mixed with melting snow for the next couple of days. They built the campfire under the wagon. They passed old Fort Hawley and could see the hay fields where the two men had been killed, but where they had found only one body.

The final day out, they pulled across the Gumbo Flats, where the mud balled up on the wagon wheels until they had to be dug out at regular intervals. When Jim stepped down to clean off the wheels, the gumbo stuck to his boots and they got bigger and heavier with each step.

At last they arrived at the site of the Musselshell. Jim stopped their wagon on a clear running creek a short distance from the Missouri. The Missouri was running high as it roared by. The water was black with huge hunks of ice, uprooted trees and logs. Not much had been built there except for a couple of crude cabins and a larger building, which was to be the trading post. Jim went to the post and found Norris, Halpin and Martin, as well as Captain Andrews from the Montana Hide and Fur Company and Colonel Clendennin from the T.C. Power Company. He and Maggie were greeted with excitement and were told that one of the cabins was for them.

The men also told him that they had been continually hit by Indians and most of the horses were gone. Jim felt that with a good stockade, the stock could be protected.

The summer before had not been the best. They had low water all season, and boats were not able to get to Fort Benton. The boats had to leave freight at the Musselshell, but the Musselshell didn't have any stock to haul the freight because the Sioux had stolen all the horses and mules. The day the first steamboat stopped, a small band of Sioux crawled through the sagebrush and cut loose the last horse in the settlement. It was an iron-hobbled horse close to a cabin. The Indians couldn't get it loose with the hobble on, but one of the whites shot the horse in the fight. The Crows had lots of horses in their camp and the Sioux were taking those also, as the two tribes were fighting each other. So Jim had the only team, which made it possible to haul logs for his cabin and stockade.

Within a few weeks Jim's stockade started to take shape.

He built his cabin on the creek, which Maggie named "Jim Wells Creek."

Early one morning Little Mac showed up in camp. Jim was out notching logs when he heard: "Wells — got yourself a nice stockade here."

Jim turned in surprise. "What're you doing out here, Mac? Thought you were getting rich in the gold mines."

"I couldn't take that easy life so I went back to wolfing and got me a wagonload, but no wagon."

"Well, maybe I can help you if I can talk you into working with me here at the post."

"Jim, you are still the trader and to look at your place, you're going to put the rest out of business. I should settle down for awhile. How's Maggie?"

"She's fine; let's go take a coffee break and let her see you."

Maggie was as beautiful as ever to Mac, and the cabin was warm and smelled good, with a big pot of coffee over the fire. Maggie didn't recognize him at first with his beard. But as soon as she did, she gave him a big hug of welcome. "It's good to see you again. Will you stay awhile?"

"Jim's offered me a job. I'll have to go to work for him so I can use his wagon to get my winter wolf hides in before they spoil. Jim, you hoping for a big year here at Musselshell?"

"Yes, Mac. New team and wagons will be arriving soon, and I plan to do lots of trading with the Gros Ventres."

"Jim, when can I get that wagon of yours?"

"You can take it tomorrow. I got plenty of logs already cut and down to keep me busy for a week."

The Musselshell was about as primitive as all the other trading posts. The men lived mostly on game, occasionally hauling in an eel or a catfish. For a special treat they might stir up some flour and make dough; dough fried in bacon grease was even better. Dough was also popular baked in sagebrush

embers or wrapped around a stick and roasted over a fire of
buffalo chips. Maggie could no longer cook for everyone but
there was always someone hanging around their cabin hoping
to be invited in for dinner.

Tobacco never lasted out the winter, so those who liked a
smoke took up the Indian method of stretching tobacco with
willow bark, creating a blend known as kinnikinnick.

Along with a number of trappers, traders and frontiersmen,
women from different tribes frequented the Musselshell. Some
came for the night, retreating to the Indian camps by day;
others lived there in the post. One day a white woman dressed
in skins came to the Musselshell. Though her name was Jenny,
she was known by the men as 'The Buffalo Whore' because she
would sleep with anyone, white or Indian, for the price of a few
hides. She was fat and ugly and tough; she had to be to survive.

One day, Jenny and a Crow woman left the Fort to collect
kindling. They did this on a regular basis, but this morning a
Sioux was hiding in the sagebrush and shot at them. The Crow
was wounded, Jenny was not. She could have escaped but
instead tried to help the Crow make it back into the Fort. The
Sioux shot again, this time hitting Jenny. Jim, hearing her
screams, dashed out of his cabin in time to see the Sioux tearing
Jenny's scalp from her head. Jim fired, killing one of the Sioux
as the other ran off with her red hair in his hand. Jenny and
the Crow woman were carried back into the Fort. Everyone
thought they would die, but Maggie stayed with them and
both recovered.

Early one spring morning, nearly fifty men were waiting
around the settlement. It had been said that the first
steamboat of the season was on its way upstream. The water
was so low that the men anticipated a busy, profitable summer
hauling freight away from the unnavigable river.

Jim was proud of his stockade and trading was good. He would be pleased when the boat arrived at the Musselshell, bringing more supplies. And one of the first things he was going to find was a wig for Jenny to wear. She was not the most beautiful woman in the first place, but now with that big bald spot, she was nothing to admire.

That day, a group of Crow women went out to gather firewood. Shots rang out from the cliff over the river, and sent the women screaming back to the fort.

The men, who were anticipating the arrival of the steamboat, were well armed and in large numbers to guard the trading post. They burst from the fort and some started to chase the dozen or so Sioux. One of the men who worked at the fort with Jim, Jake Leader, was shot down and killed. Some of the men were frightened and ran back to the fort; Jim and several of the others were too angry to do anything but forge ahead.

Bushway suggested to Jim that they try and draw the Indians' fire. So for several hours, Jim and the men tried every tactic to make the Indians shoot, but nothing worked. At last it began to rain, and Jim realized that with their breech-loading rifles, they had the advantage over the Indians with their flintlock guns.

The men finally decided on a plan — to cross the shallow Musselshell River and fire directly into the coulee from behind the brush on the opposite shore. Little Mac and two others volunteered. As the men waded across, they turned and saw the Indians trying in every way they could to shoot them down. But the rain ruined the effect of the guns and of the bows.

The other men were taller than Little Mac and wore buckskin shirts only. As they crossed, the water was up to Little Mac's armpits, and he was dressed completely in buckskins. As his pants got wet they started to stretch and made walking impossible, so he had to kick them off. This left Mac with the memorable experience of coming ashore to fight the Indians with nothing on but his shirt.

When they reached the other side, the men peered through the willows and saw that the coulee contained nearly 200 Sioux, completely naked and covered with war paint.

Suddenly, Jim and the two other men from the stockade came around to join them, guns ready. When all men were in position, they started to fire.

The war party was trapped. Some immediately recognized the hopelessness of the situation, and began to wail their death song. Others sprang from the ravine and were met with a volley of fire. Some plunged into the Musselshell and were shot in the water; others dragged themselves into the brush. It was a complete massacre. Finally, when all was still, a young half-breed boy ran from the coulee, surrendering himself.

One of the hunters from the fort shot him down instantly, and without a moment's hesitation, slit open the boy's chest and removed his liver. He then held up the warm liver and took an enormous bite. He offered some to the others.

Jim almost threw up. From that day on, everyone called the hunter "Liver-Eating Johnson." Jim also caught Johnson cutting a strip of skin from a dead Indian.

"What are you doing with that?"

"I'm making myself a razor strop."

Jim was appalled by another man, Captain Andrews. He cut off heads, removed the flesh and brains by boiling, and labeled the skulls with names.

"Andrews," Mac asked. "What are you planning to do with them skulls when you're through?"

"I'm going to tour the United States and give lectures," responded Andrews.

The day after, Jim and some of the men found the ravine where the Sioux had stripped for their ambush. There they discovered over a hundred robes, dozens of moccasins and two war bonnets. Jim and Little Mac were given the war bonnets for their bravery. Jim thanked everyone, but the killing of the Indians, even to protect the fort, gave him a bitter, sick feeling.

After this battle at the Musselshell, the fort settled down to trading, but the Indians continued to harass the settlement. There was no mass ambush, but they continued to steal horses and burn buildings and woodpiles.

It was a hard year and the dream of a new route to Helena was starting to fail. Wagons were attacked by the Sioux. By early fall it was decided to close down the post. Jim and Maggie were to go back to Fort Benton.

George Clendennin decided to stay on at the stockade and continue trade with the friendly Gros Ventres and Crows. He borrowed a cannon from Fort Buford for protection. The Indians feared the cannon most and would avoid an attack if they knew the fort had one. George Clendennin renamed the Musselshell "Fort Sheridan."

Jim and Maggie loaded their wagon and started the familiar trip back to Fort Benton. "It's going to be hard to leave this place, Maggie. I finally got a home built for you, and now we move on again."

"I keep telling you, Jim, we should live in a tipi. It's a lot easier to pack up and move. I'm not looking forward to living in Fort Benton."

"Maggie, I'm sure it will only be for a short time and then we'll get another trading post."

They were able to find the Gros Ventre camp and spend a couple of days with Maggie's family. Jim was always happy in camp. He loved to be out in the open and away from the rotten smells of the trading posts, but he was a trader and knew he would be back in a post before long.

CHAPTER NINE

The Judith

Jim knew Fort Benton would be their home until he could find a new trading post. He and Maggie were able to find a small white house with glass windows just off the main street. Their second day back in town, Jim headed over to the fur company to find out what his new tasks would be. Mr. Power informed him that he would be traveling around to all the different posts, giving advice and support. In other words, he would be the new troubleshooter.

Later that day Jim spotted Little Mac. "Thought I might see you around here," Jim said, glad to find his friend again, shaking his hand.

"Jim! You know, I tried some mining again but I'm getting too old to be worrying about losing my scalp every five minutes. Now I have a job working for T.C. Power, sorting and baling buffalo robes. Lots of the boys are here at Benton — seems like this is always going to be the main port. Got your new job yet?"

"Yeah, I'm going to be the new troubleshooter for the fur company. I'll be making rounds of all the posts."

"Why don't you meet me after work at the saloon?" Little Mac said. "You can see some of the boys."

"Sounds good. Where are you living, Mac? Maggie and I found a little house over on the next street."

"I have a room at the Overland Hotel." The Overland Hotel was an oversized log cabin with some rough-framed additions.

"Good. I'll see you later this afternoon."

Thinking about all those bales of buffalo hides, Jim knew that the Indians wondered about the mysterious disappearance of the buffalo from their accustomed range. They were all seeing the once millions of buffalo dwindling down to thousands, and in some areas only isolated small bands.

Jim showed up at the saloon that afternoon. Little Mac waved to him from across the room.

"Glad you could make it, Jim. Want you to meet Flossie. You know Seven-Up and the rest of the boys from the Pony Express."

"I sure do. Looks like you got a homecoming here."

"Let me buy you a whiskey, Jim. You want another, Flossie?"

As Jim looked around he could see a few dance hall girls in their colorful dresses. "It's nice to see white women again, isn't it Jim?" Mac started out. "I mean in contrast with the squaws, these dance hall girls seem like creatures from a fairy world. They all smell like a garden, full of flowers. I don't want you to get mad; Maggie is an exception."

"It's a good thing you put that in, Mac," Jim said. To Jim, the dance hall girls looked stale and ugly compared to Maggie.

The whiskey came and a toast was given. Jim could see that Flossie was drinking doubles to their singles.

All the saloons were the same. Somebody banged on the piano, while some of the other patrons might start a square dance. There were never enough girls to go around, and those who couldn't afford a girl partner for a dance would dance with each other. It was fun to watch these big frontiersmen stomping around together.

Flossie was pretty, with high-piled hair interlaced with ribbons; her low-necked, crimson bodice glistened with spangles. She wore lots of paint and powder. Jim was glad to see Little Mac having such a good time.

"Mac, I'm going to turn in. How 'bout you coming to dinner tomorrow night."

"I'd be glad to."

"See you then."

The next evening Mac came to dinner at the Wells' place. That day Jim had learned that he would be leaving for Fort Peck on the Milk River in about a week. "You're welcome to come along," Jim told Mac.

"I appreciate it, but I want to stay around here for awhile," Mac replied. "I had some trouble with some Crows last time out, and better not press my luck."

"What happened, Mac?"

"I was traveling with six dogs and a sled, and was caught in a snowstorm. I spent the night with a tribe of Mountain Crow, and ate a delicious meal with them of pork stew. Gobbled it down I might add, and next morning discovered they'd fed me two of my own dogs. I was so angry I kicked one of them, and rode off yelling with the uneaten part of my team."

Jim laughed. "I told you, when I was sick and staying with the Gros Ventres I was fed dog meat. In fact, we were given a pregnant dog as a wedding present. Mostly the pups are eaten, not the old dogs."

"I still don't see anything wrong with eating dogs," Maggie started in, "as long as you are raising them for that purpose. It made you healthy, Jim."

"Yeah, Maggie, that's why I sound like a dog when I cough."

"I don't know if I can ever look a pup in the eye again," Mac said.

"Mac," Jim said, "when I'm out for the trading company I'll be looking for a place for my own post. The thing we need to start thinking about is the railroad. They've got terminals all along the river from St. Louis to St. Joseph, out to Bismarck in the Dakotas. A lot of old-timers think we're nuts having an idea that someday a locomotive might come roaring into Fort Benton. I think we'll both live to see the day that they do. The boat lines keep expanding, saying the railroad could never meet the rates of the steamboat. But I think they'll be able to."

"Well, that still gives you and me, Jim, a few more years of making a living off the land."

"Just think about it," Jim said.

The season started with the arrival of the first steamboat up from St. Louis. A cannon would be fired from a lookout point a few miles downstream and then it would be answered by a whistle from the steamboat. This exchange brought the inhabitants of Fort Benton running to the landing to greet the boat.

It was a good chance to see the mixture of people that populated Fort Benton. There were the grizzled, whiskered trappers, the scouts and traders with their mangey hair, Indians in blankets or buckskin, cowboy ranchers, Chinese workers, gamblers, soldiers and officers from the fort, women in bright colored dresses, town ladies in hoods and shawls, and children everywhere.

After the steamboat was tied up to a battered old cottonwood stump, down would come the gangplank and over it would pour returning businessmen, new prospectors and trappers, a few Jesuit missionaries, an officer and his wife, and possibly a few new girls who would make a living in the busy saloons. As soon as the passengers were off, down came the mules and work horses. The ship's cargo was unloaded onto the docks and the waiting furs and gold were trundled aboard the steamboat. Everyone had to move fast, since the season would last for three months at the most.

This was the steamboat Jim took down to Fort Peck. He said goodbye to Maggie and was hoping this would be a short trip, his first on a river steamboat. The steamboat seemed to move swiftly downriver with the high water of spring. They hit only one sandbar where they had to pole the boat over.

The steamboat moved only in daylight. Jim noticed that the pilot never trusted his ship to the river more than ten to twelve hours at a stretch. The moment daylight prevented him from searching out signs of trouble — such as hidden reefs and rocks — the ship was tied up along the bank or to some firm object in the current for the night.

It took a lot less wood to go downriver, about ten cords every twenty-four hours, whereas it took twenty-five to thirty cords to push a steamboat upriver. Jim knew most of the "woodhawks" along the river from Fort Benton to Fort Peck; he had cut a few cords himself.

When they arrived at Fort Peck it had not changed since the last time Jim had been there. The stockade still sprawled along a narrow shelf of bottom land. Jim departed the ship and headed toward the stockade. "Lot more Indian lodges," he thought.

It was a thriving trading post. It was Jim's job to check the books and guess what trading goods were to be sent. Joe Bushway was still in charge and seemed to have the post well organized. They were still having some trouble from the Sioux and Crow.

Jim and Joe conversed later inside the fort. "How long do you plan to stay here at Fort Peck, Jim?"

"Until I can catch another boat going to Fort Benton. Seems you're in good shape down here. I'm going to be making the rounds of all the posts this summer, then I hope to get my own post by next spring."

"You got any ideas where yet?"

"No, but I hope it's better than Musselshell."

"The Musselshell's still going. Maybe you moved out too fast."

"No, Joe, that place'll be gone in a couple of years, just like your place if you don't get back from this river. One day high water's going to take you."

"You know, that creek's still got your name on it — Jim Wells Creek."

"That's about all they're going to remember of my time down there."

Jim did his work at the fort. He went around to see if he knew any of the Gros Ventres, but all were from different groups. He noticed the Indians looking poorer all the time.

Jim had dinner with Joe. A boat was expected the next day, so Jim would be on his way back to Fort Benton. Jim said, "You know, Little Mac is in Fort Benton. I had supper with him just before I came down here. He tried gold mining. Now he's working for T.C. Power." Jim told Joe the story about Mac eating the dog, and about his girlfriend Flossie. He told him that a lot of the boys from the Pony Express were in Fort Benton now.

Jim was happy to see the boat arrive the next evening. It exchanged supplies, took on wood and then left at dawn the next day. Everyone from Fort Peck was out to wave the steamboat off. But what caught Jim's eye on the way back was a beautiful piece of bottom land where the Judith River emptied into the Missouri. There he saw a large, grassy island which they had to go around in the river. Jim thought it would be a great spot for a trading post and for raising cattle — and maybe for raising a family as well.

The only thing that had changed in Fort Benton in the short time Jim was gone was that the levees were piled higher with freight: barrels of salt, flour, dried apples, crackers, mining machinery, furniture, lots of whiskey kegs, buggies, dogs, pigs, horses, crates of chickens, sacks of coffee beans, tobacco. As Jim's boat pulled towards the mooring he could see Maggie waiting on the crowded levee. He was such a lucky man to have her as his wife. As soon as the gangplank landed, he was off and heading for her. He gave her a big hug and kiss. "I sure missed you, Maggie. It was only a couple of weeks but it seems like I've been gone such a long time."

"It seemed like a long time to me too, Jim. I wasn't sure what boat you would be on so I have met them all."

"How has Benton been treating you, Maggie?"

"It's not bad for me, but I feel sorry for all the other Indians who can't get served in the store, when I walk in and charge anything."

"I hope not anything!"

"Yes, Jim, I could have anything."

"Ah, Maggie. I see my bags on the levee."

Jim grabbed his bags and they headed home. Maggie had been busy with the house since he left. She had cleaned and redecorated, putting up new curtains.

"Maggie, the cabin looks great. Where did you get some of this furniture?"

"From people who were leaving and couldn't take everything. You like these things?"

"I sure do. You have done wonders with this place."

Jim spent the next month traveling around from post to post, and on these trips he took Maggie. Since most posts were inland, they rode with the freight wagons or took their own wagon loaded with supplies.

One day in the fall, when Jim and Maggie returned from a trip, Jim had a message from T.C. Power saying that Power wanted to meet with him as soon as possible. Jim sent a note over saying he could meet the next morning.

Jim walked down to the trading post in the morning.

"Jim, come right in," T.C. Power greeted him. "You want coffee?"

"Yes, please."

"Sit down, Jim. I'll get right to the point. I want to hire you as my agent down at Fort Clagget. We're going to try and bypass Fort Benton again."

Jim was surprised. "I'd like to be your agent. But I also want to be your partner in that venture," countered Jim.

"Well, I never thought of that, but a partner usually works harder. Think this might work where Musselshell failed. Jim, give me a day or two to think about that partnership."

"That's fine with me. I would also like to hire Little Mac for down there."

"You got the money for a partnership, Jim?"

"I reckon so. Tell you the truth, I like that land down at the Judith and the Missouri. "

"All right, Jim. We'll meet in a couple of days."

Jim rushed home and told Maggie his news.

"Maggie, T.C. Power wants me as agent down at Fort Clagget. You remember, near the site of old Camp Cooke, at the junction of the Judith, the place where you and I met, or should I say, the winter camp for the Gros Ventres."

"Do you think you will take the job?"

"Only if I become a partner. I'd also like to start a ranch there."

"Sounds like you're looking for a place to settle down, Jim."

"Maybe with the railroad coming and all the changes, we have to start out on our own."

Maggie smiled. "When will you know?"

"T.C. Power said the next couple of days. Hate to move you out of here just as you settled in."

"Jim, I spent most of my life moving three or four times a year."

A couple of days later, Jim received a note from T.C. Power. He asked for a meeting that afternoon. When Jim arrived, Power was waiting for him and took him into the office. "Well, Jim, ready to get down to business?"

"I sure am."

"I want you to be our agent, and I'm willing to sell you a half share in that fort and whatever we develop down there."

"Sounds good. What do you figure this partnership is worth?"

"You'll be doing all the work. We would set you up with stock. I figure twenty-five hundred would be fair for both, then we split the profits."

"That sounds more than fair to me. You draw up the papers and I'll sign."

"You know, Jim, this may be a big flop, or, we might make a few dollars."

"I know, but I got to take a chance somewhere. Why not the Clagget?"

"You've got what it takes, Jim. Oh, and by the way, there is one other thing I want to mention to you."

"What's that?"

"Your wife, Maggie — is she a Gros Ventre?"

"She is," Jim said. "What about it?"

"You know, Jim, that if anything were to happen to you, you

would not be able to pass along any property to Maggie because she's an Indian? I didn't make the law — I think the law is abominable. I'm only mentioning this because it's important for us to discuss it as partners. I wouldn't want your wife to end up penniless. Perhaps we could make some kind of trustee arrangement so that Maggie would be well taken care of. It's dangerous out there, Jim. You know better than anyone."

Jim nodded. He hadn't let himself think about anything like this, but if he were getting into a partnership maybe he ought to. "I appreciate what you're saying. I'll think about that too."

"Good," Power said.

The two men shook hands and Jim knew it was going to be a long friendship and partnership.

When Jim opened the door to his house, he said, "Well, Maggie, I'm in a partnership and we're going to Clagget."

"Oh, I'm so glad! How soon will we be leaving Fort Benton?"

"Don't know yet, Maggie. Should know in a couple of days. You'll have plenty of notice. How'd you like to go over to Perkins' place for dinner and celebrate?"

Dinner at Perkins' was fun and a lot busier. "I remember when John and I would come in here and be the only ones for dinner. You sure are busy now," Jim said to Perkins.

"As the town grows, we still have the best food and you know I'll always make room for you and Maggie, even if I have to throw a couple of those frontiersmen out to get you a space."

"I'm leaving Fort Benton again, Perkins. Going down to Fort Clagget to set up a new trading post for T.C. Power. This time I'm going to be a partner."

"You always have a place to stay when you come up here. In fact, that isn't such a far trip."

Walking back to their house, Maggie looked at Jim and

said, "I'm glad to be leaving. Did you see the way people looked at me as if to say, 'What's an Indian doing in an eating place?'"

"Maggie, I told you, just throw some food at them, and say, 'Excuse me, I'm just a savage.'"

"Jim, you know it does bother me."

"I know, Maggie. I wish it wasn't like this."

"I know you do."

Jim was aware that they were still in a territory where most whites felt that the only good Indian was a dead Indian, and where men would trade their Indian wives as if they were trading goods.

Jim spent the next week signing papers — including a trust for Maggie, with Power as Trustee — and getting supplies ready to move to the Judith. The more he worked on the project, the more excited he became. He talked to Little Mac who decided to come along with them. Mac was lost without Flossie in Fort Benton.

The word was out about the new fort, and as usual there were as many sceptics as those who thought it would succeed. All could remember the Musselshell and didn't want that to happen again.

Jim and Maggie loaded their belongings in the wagon. By the end of the second week, Jim was ready to start for the Judith. As they pulled out of Fort Benton, Jim hoped that the Judith would prove to be their home for a while.

Jim enjoyed the time on the trail with Maggie. He was able to shoot a couple of deer, one for fresh meat and one for drying. He saved the hides for Maggie to use later.

When they made it to the Judith, Jim spent a couple of days selecting a good spot for his trading post. He finally chose a spot about 200 yards on the eastern side of the Judith River. He felt boats could pull off the Missouri River and tie up in the calmer waters of the Judith. He decided to build this post out of stone so as not to have trouble with fires and rotting timbers. It would be one hundred feet long and twenty feet wide, with docks out over the water.

People were starting to come to the area, so he was able to hire help and construction began. He put corrals to one side and started his house to the rear of the trading post. Trading started right up, so he had a supply of hides when the first boat arrived. Within four months, the post and the house were finished and it had grown to a community of about sixty people.

By fall, wagons were moving on a regular basis towards Helena and the interior. The post wasn't that big, but if it could function a month earlier in the spring and a month later in the fall, it could become important.

They were losing a few wagons to the Indians, but not as many as they had expected.

Jim spent a lot of his spare time checking out the area for his ranch. The most important thing was water — if he controlled the water, he controlled the land. If he staked out some land he would go to Texas in the fall and drive some cattle back by spring. And the Judith looked like an ideal place to start his cattle ranch: good grass, water and protection in the winter. Finally he drew a map of the area and marked out a block eight miles north and south on the Judith and fourteen miles around the south bank of the Missouri. He filed a claim in his own name and that of T.C. Power.

Jim thought if he could start the herd north in the warmer winter down south, he could get it to the Judith before calving began. He figured he could keep a head of 500 to 600 in this area easily. He couldn't understand why cattle had not been brought to the Judith area already.

Overall, the summer of 1871 was a good one. The post had done a lot more business than anyone had hoped for. Jim did more trading with the Gros Ventres and saw more of Maggie's tribe. (They still produced the best hides.) And Jim staked out fields that could be cut for hay and set up corrals that could be used for winter feeding to prepare for his herd.

The best news was that Maggie was pregnant with their first child. Jim and Maggie decided that Jim would go and hire a Gros Ventre woman to live with them and help while Jim was away; and also to help with the delivery in the spring. It would be hard for Jim to leave for Texas after cattle, but in the long run it would be better if he went now.

Jim left early one morning. He was sure he would find the Gros Ventres near the Milk River. He should be able to make it in a couple of days, as he was anxious to return quickly.

It took Jim two and a half days to find the camp. He couldn't believe how poor it looked. Old hides on tipis weren't replaced, and most of the dogs were gone.

He rode up to Horse Capture's tipi. He was greeted with a big hug as he dismounted his horse. "Welcome, Jim. It has been a long time."

"I have some news for you, Capture," Jim said. "Maggie's going to have a baby. I'm here to see if Maggie's mother, or anyone else, might like to come live with us for awhile to help Maggie out."

Capture smiled. "This is very good. Congratulations, Jim. But I have some sad news — Maggie's mother died this last winter. We lost many in our band. Come sit, Jim, and smoke with me."

As Jim sat down he felt lost. Why, why must the white man destroy these beautiful people? The Gros Ventres had always wanted to work with the whites, but the whites just grabbed more and more.

Capture lit the pipe, blew smoke, and pulled it around himself in a blessing. He handed it to Jim, who did the same.

"Now, Jim, that you are blessed by the smoke of the pipe, we can talk business. I will find you a good woman to help with the birth and stay with Maggie."

"Thank you, Capture. I'll be gone for many months and I want to get back to Maggie soon."

"Jim, we will have a sweat and feast tonight and you can leave tomorrow. Come, let me show you our camp."

Jim still knew many of the tribe, and they greeted him with loud yells.

Capture had the sweat lodge made ready. Jim and about a dozen men piled in. Capture and a helper passed rocks heated outside on the fork of a stick, one by one, while those inside prayed and sang. Jim prayed that his baby would be healthy and be part of this proud group. The entrance flap was then closed and cold water poured over the stones. In the enveloping cloud of steam, the worshippers could hear the voice of the spirit. Jim could feel the wing of the eagle brushing over his back and a voice telling him he would have a son. He then rubbed himself with sage leaves.

When they came out of the sweat lodge at the end of the afternoon, they walked down to the Milk River to wash in its cold water. As Jim slid into the river he prepared for the first shock, but it was very soothing. His clothes were on the bank waiting for him. As he stood on the bank dressing, he felt refreshed and relaxed.

"Jim, when you are dressed we will eat." Capture's voice brought him back to reality.

"Thank you, Capture. That was a good sweat."

As they sat around the fire, Jim's food was brought to him first. He could see that the whole camp would share in that one steer, and nothing would go to waste.

Capture spoke. "It is hard without the buffalo, Jim. He gave us everything. The meat of your beef is sweet with no fat, and the hide is small and will not last like our buffalo. It is the plan of the white man to kill all the buffalo, then the Indian will starve and beg for his food. We will not be free," Capture went on. "The Army is trying to put us on one piece of land that we cannot leave, and we are too small to fight and our food will soon be gone."

Jim knew what he was hearing was true, and he knew that the Gros Ventres only wanted to live in peace. They could speak English and many, such as Maggie, were educated by the missionaries. These proud people would be gone.

Jim was relaxed and tired. "Capture, I'm ready to sleep."

"Come, Jim, I will give you a robe."

Jim entered the tipi and could see that a spot had been prepared for him. He said his goodnights and rolled up in his buffalo robe with his back to the fire. He thought back to how these people had saved his life.

He slept late the next morning, and found that camp activity was already moving. He was served some of the meat from the night before. Capture came in as he was finishing. "Jim, I found you a good woman. She lost her husband this last winter and can't find a new one. She is here to meet you."

"Thank you, Capture."

An young Indian woman entered the tipi and stood beside Capture.

"Jim, this is Na-min-na."

"Blue Sky — that's a nice name."

"She speaks no English so you must speak Gros Ventre or Sioux." She would not look up at Jim. "She has worked with the woman who delivers the babies and is strong and can help Maggie. When she is finished you can keep her there or send her back to the camp."

"Capture, if you say she is good, she is good. Does she have any children?"

"She had a son who died in the winter with its father. And as you know, she must find a new husband to support her and no one can afford more than one wife. And some of the men want none, so she has survived by begging."

"How long will it take her to get ready to leave? She can have my extra horse."

"Jim, she is ready."

"Capture, I thank you for your hospitality, but I want to start back as soon as possible. I want to stop by and see Cyprenne Matt, that French trader from Quebec. He has a Gros Ventre wife. He buys supplies from me."

"I remember Cyprenne Matt — his wife's from the other clan. Good trader, but not as good as you, Jim."

Jim was on the trail by noon and figured he could make Matt's trading post by noon the next day. He stopped early so a camp could be set up. Blue Sky had the camp and fire going before Jim had taken care of the horses. She prepared a stew and hard Indian bread. She was able to make coffee, to Jim's surprise.

"Blue Sky, that was a good meal. The coffee was a surprise to me."

"My husband liked the white man's coffee."

They were up early, had leftovers from the previous night's dinner, and were on the trail early. They arrived at Matt's trading post that evening. Matt's post was small and he traded flour, sugar, tea, baking powder, whiskey, ammunition, beads, calico and blankets to the Indians for furs. The huge herds of buffalo had been slaughtered and the furs were mostly wolf. The going price was $2.50 for wolf, $1.25 for coyote, $5.00 for lynx, $1.50 for bobcat, and $1.25 for fox. Matt's prices changed — like most traders, he gauged them by the Indians' need and desire for the goods. A good example was given to Jim: one sky-blue bead, costing about sixty cents a gross, might be traded for a buffalo robe, but other colors were worth nothing. The colors had meaning. If a warrior wore a blue bead into battle and was not hurt, it was the protection of the bead, and then all the warriors wanted that color.

Jim and Blue Sky were greeted by a couple of Matt's kids and his wife Melanie. It wasn't long before Cyprenne himself was at the door. "Mr. Wells, welcome. Welcome to my post. You have a new wife?"

"No, this is Blue Sky, and she's going back to the Judith to help Maggie, who is having a baby."

"Congratulations! Come in, Jim, come in."

Dinner was ready and a couple more plates were put on the table, along with an extra glass filled with whiskey for Jim. "To your health, Jim."

"And to yours."

Jim could feel his head getting light. He drank too much — he couldn't remember going to bed and had a very large head the next morning.

In the morning, Jim and Blue Sky said their goodbyes and were back on the trail. Jim didn't feel good and wished he had stayed away from the whiskey. They made it back to the Judith late that evening.

Maggie was at the door to greet Jim. She remembered Blue Sky and greeted her with joy. Jim went right to bed. He woke a few times to hear the chatter of Maggie and Blue Sky. They must have talked all night.

Early the next morning, he knew he had to talk to Maggie. When he told her that her mother had died during the winter, she didn't say a word. But that afternoon she packed some things and prepared to go to the hills for a couple of days. Jim wanted to talk her out of it because he was afraid she would be in danger, but he had vowed from the beginning not to prevent Maggie from maintaining any of her customs, and now he had to stick to his word.

In early fall, Jim and Maggie were visited by Father Giorda. He was still the General Superior of the missions and had his headquarters at St. Mary's. Maggie was excited to see him and invited him to their home. "Father, it is so good to see you. Are you going to have a Mass here at the Judith for the Catholics?"

"Of course. You look very good, Maggie. Jim is treating you well?"

"Father, Jim is a wonderful man, and a real protector of me. Awhile back a man made a pass at me, and Jim almost took his hand off with an axe handle. The word got around fast. Father, the good news is that I will have a baby in the spring."

"That's wonderful. Will I get to baptize the baby?"

"Oh, yes. We'll bring it to you."

Walking in the door, Jim said, "Father, welcome to the Judith. I see the Indians haven't grabbed your hair yet."

"Almost, though. Last year I was at my desk and an Indian shot at me through the window. Good thing he was tipsy or I would be dead."

"Your Jesuit God has been with you. How long will you be here?"

"Just one day, Jim. I want to say Mass tomorrow and be on my way."

"You can stay here — we have an extra room."

"I would be pleased to stay."

Many stories were passed back and forth that night between Jim and Father Giorda. The next morning the Father said Mass in front of the cabin for the frontiersmen and Indians; then again he was on his way.

Jim marveled at how people came and went, in and out of their lives here in the Territory. "It was good to see him again, wasn't it, Maggie?"

"Yes, Jim. I told him he could baptize our baby."

"Forgive me if I'm not back by then, Maggie."

"I know you'll be back."

Jim held Maggie against him as tightly as he could. No matter what he worried about, he still felt like the luckiest man in the world.

CHAPTER TEN

Down the River

It was late august when Jim kissed Maggie goodbye and boarded the river boat. It was harder for Jim to leave than ever before. The boat was owned by T.C. Power and carried a letter for Jim, wishing him good luck, and his share of cash to make the trip and buy cattle. Inside he was greeted by the captain and given a cabin reserved for first-class passengers. The captain informed Jim that the trip took two weeks at the most, five weeks to come back. As the boat cast off, Jim stood on the deck, waving goodbye to Maggie and Little Mac. He prayed everything would be all right while he was away.

Jim wished John was with him. This was an adventure his brother would have enjoyed.

The boat moved out into the middle of the river and picked up speed and the Judith disappeared as they rounded a bend. It was a long, boring day for Jim, who had always been busy at the trading post.

The boat tied up at the Musselshell the first night so Jim was able to walk around to see what was left of his post. He finally found George Clendennin in his warehouse, cutting hides to ship out on the boat.

"Jim, what are you doing down here?"

"I'm on the river boat — heading south to get some cattle."

"Well, as you can see, I'm still here. Trading keeps dropping off. Probably have to close in a couple of years."

"George, you want to have dinner with me on the boat? I'd like to hear how things are going with you."

"Sure, Jim. I'll be done here about eight o'clock. I'll get cleaned up and see you about eight forty-five."

"Sounds good."

Jim found the place where his cabin had been. The ground was still packed down. He did find a sign by the creek, "Jim Wells Creek." It made him laugh. He had his mark on history if the creek didn't dry up and disappear.

George showed up for dinner right at the marked time. "Jim, it's a pleasure to have dinner on the boat. I still have to eat my own cooking. Tell me about the Judith."

"I had a good year, and built me a trading post out of stone this time. It should last longer than the one I had here. And I put a claim on some land. Going to Texas to bring back a herd so I can raise some beef."

"Smart, Jim. Getting your fingers in more pies."

"You know the thing that will change everything is if they put in that railroad past Bismarck."

After dinner they parted, saying that they would see each other in the spring.

The boat pulled out at the first sign of dawn. The workers spent most of the night taking on hides and wood for the day's trip. Jim wondered when the men slept, working the boat all day and loading wood at night. They were lucky the water was flowing deep and fast, but Jim also knew it would seem shallower as they went downriver and the load grew heavier.

Jim wondered what the next stop would be; from Fort Peck it would be all new territory. The captain kept telling Jim how lucky they were. Usually by August it was low water and no passage, but the flow had stayed up. Around the Yellowstone, the Missouri often narrowed and the river looked like it had been sucked out. The crew had to "walk" the ship across the dry sand bars inch by inch, foot by foot, yard by yard.

The country looked lonely from the river, with its high dry bluffs, and only once in a while a lone Indian or rider. The Mackinaws were still on the river for their one-way trip down the Missouri. Mackinaws were boats that hauled a large load downriver and then were taken apart and sold for lumber at their destination. Jim could hear the swearing as the steamboat passed one, rocking it on its wave. But the Mackinaws could glide across the shallow sand bars while the steamboat had to be walked.

Jim was surprised at how many men he recognized on those boats as frontiersmen trying to get a better price for their hides by taking them downriver themselves, getting out of the territory for the winter.

Jim started to feel lonesome as he got farther from Maggie and the Judith.

That night they pulled in after dark at Fort Peck. It looked to Jim as if half of Fort Peck had gone down the Missouri in the spring. It was still a small, ugly post and he wondered why they built it on that narrow shelf, which was more narrow now, with those naked yellow cliffs behind the fort that took all protection away. He could remember stories about Indians standing on top and shooting down into the stockade. It wasn't his fort and he never liked coming down to visit. One thing was sure, the Missouri would take it before the Indians.

He didn't even get off the boat at Fort Peck. He had dinner and turned in for the night.

From there the river narrowed. Jim thought that if it were narrower the water would be deep and move faster, but for some reason he didn't understand, it became shallower and slower. They only got as far as Fort Kipp, which was just another woodchoppers' stop.

Late the next day, they came to where the Yellowstone entered the Missouri and the water level increased again. The land was becoming more barren but as barren as it was, it was still beautiful.

It was interesting to Jim to see all the wood stops and how the steamboats provided a living for the choppers. At each stop the boat was secured on an old rotting stump. How many times had boats been secured at each dock, he wondered. The stumps looked like they couldn't hold a boat for the night.

A couple of Mackinaws were tied up at this stop, as well as a few bull boats. The Indians would construct a circular or oval-shaped basket of willow poles, lashed in place with strips of rawhide that had been stretched over the frame. They stretched tough bull buffalo hides, hair side out and usually with the tail left on, then sewed them together with sinew for thread. Then the boat was put in the hot sun to shrink the hides as tight as a drum. Everyday the outside was smeared with ashes and tallow, to prevent the hides from rotting. The thing that amazed Jim was that the boat was so light a child could carry one. Yet they were so sturdy that they could carry a ton or more of furs, and two could paddle them. It was interesting to see the innovation of man to move supplies there.

In a couple more days they arrived at Bismarck. This was a fast-moving city; it was also the end or the beginning of the railroad, depending on which way you were moving. The steamboat unloaded a lot of its cargo here for shipment to the east. The town had hotels, shops, public rating houses and public baths. It was the biggest city Jim had seen in years.

Jim decided to have dinner in town. The place he picked had white tablecloths and real silver. It was one fancy place and expensive — the whole dinner cost Jim two and one-half dollars, and a beer was thirty cents.

After dinner he walked up and down the streets. He was thinking that this is what a railroad brings. At the rail yards, trains were being loaded with the hides and cattle for shipment east. This sure was a moving city.

The next morning when the steamboat moved again, it moved faster since a big part of its load was left in Bismarck.

Jim was starting to hear a new language on the river. He would hear about a "sawyer," which was a dislodged tree with roots or branches caught in the river bottom and whose trunk sawed up and down in the current. This could be a disaster to any boat it struck or pierced. Even worse than a "sawyer" was a "sleeping sawyer," a hidden disaster.

A "crossing" was when the river had consumed one bank as far as it could. Then the river would turn abruptly in the other direction to tear at the opposite shore. The steamboat would have to follow the channel broadside to the upper current, which was flowing straight ahead. "Reaches," on the other hand, were stretches of pleasant water. The "bends" all had numbers, and some had names such as Pelican Bend, Big Bend or Disaster Bend. The bends were deceiving. If you stood on top of a cliff you could see across the bend a mile and a half to two miles, but the river took twenty-five to thirty miles to make that distance.

It took another ten days to reach St. Louis. This was also a big city, the last stopping point for those going west.

There Jim changed boats from his Missouri steamboat to a Mississippi paddle wheel. The paddle wheel boats were much bigger and cleaner. His passage had been arranged and he was taken to his berth, a large room with a bed, table and chairs.

That night when he went to dinner, he felt out of place in his buckskin since most of the men wore suits. But it would have to do, since this was all he had and he wasn't about to buy a suit just for dinner. The boat also had a saloon with entertainment and gambling. It was like a little town on the river. The trip down the Mississippi River would be faster, since these boats traveled nights. They should be in Vicksburg in about four days.

The Mississippi was one big water road. It was hard to believe that a river could be so wide with so much flat land on both sides. The number of boats moving up and down the river was something, and all could pass in both directions with no problem.

The paddle boat would pull in and out of towns loading and unloading supplies, always at a fast pace. As the boat traveled farther south, all the workers became black. Jim had only seen a couple of blacks in San Francisco, and a few with the Army. There were so many along the river. Since the Civil War they were all free and none were slaves. However, you could see it was a poor living for them. Most had ragged clothes and no shoes, and all looked hungry. All were hard workers. As soon as the gangplank was down everyone worked at a run, which had to be hard in the heat that intensified as they went south. Jim's buckskin was also growing hotter as the air became heavier. He found himself in a constant sweat.

One day he was standing at the rail trying to catch a breeze off the river when the man next to him said, "You think it's hot here — wait until New Orleans. You can cut the air with a knife."

"I hope to get off in Vicksburg, catch the stage west, get back to the dry heat."

"I'm John Harding from St. Louis."

"I'm Jim Wells from Judith in Montana Territory."

"Where are you going, Jim?"

"I'm going to Texas to get a herd to take back up to the Judith."

"Where is the Judith?"

"Up near Fort Benton. I've got a trading post and some land."

"I'm a trader, but mostly household goods and furniture, made in the East and shipped out to customers along the Mississippi. How long you think it will take you to get a herd that far?"

"Tell you the truth, Mr. Harding, I don't know. Never made that trip before."

"Can I buy you dinner tonight, Mr. Wells?"

"Call me Jim. I've been eating in my cabin. People don't like my buckskin, it smells a lot like the West."

"Jim, I'd be proud to have you as my guest, even in your buckskin. See you about eight o'clock."

"Sounds good."

It was a pleasant evening. John Harding talked of how he had traveled the West, but his West had only been east of the Mississippi. Jim told him that if he ever made it to the Fort Benton area he should look him up — everyone knew how to find him. John gave Jim his card with a New York address. He said, "The best time is spring. Summer's too hot and winter's too cold, so I travel then."

The next morning they pulled in to Vicksburg, and Jim headed for the stage company. "You got a stage for Fort Worth and San Antonio?"

"Sure do. Leaves at seven a.m. tomorrow, right on time. Four days to Fort Worth, another four to San Antonio."

"I'll take a ticket."

Vicksburg was a hot, sticky swamp town. Jim was able to locate a hotel where a small breeze blew off the river. That night it rained the hardest Jim had ever seen. The drops were the size of walnuts. The thing that amazed him was that no matter how hard it rained, it was still hot.

When he woke the next day the weather had cleared. He packed and was at the stage line on time. The clerk was right; the stage pulled out promptly at seven. The road was full of holes and the holes full of water, so the side curtains had to be drawn or the passengers would get faces full of muddy water.

In the stage were six adults and one five-year-old, who had to sit on her mother's lap. The father looked like a preacher. Then there were two other men, one all dressed up in a suit like a businessman. The other looked like a cattleman, accompanied by a young woman half his age. She was pretty, with olive skin and big blue-green eyes, a color he had never seen before.

Jim was lucky; he had an outside seat and could put his head in the corner and fall asleep, if his head didn't get knocked through the side of the coach. He nodded right off.

When he woke, he looked at his pocket watch. He had slept almost two hours. The girl and the rancher were asleep next to Jim. She had her head on Jim's shoulder. The little girl was asleep across the laps of her parents. The preacher was reading the Bible.

"You a preacher?" Jim asked.

"Yes, sir. I've been assigned to a church in Fort Worth. My name's James."

"I'm James also, from Montana Territory. This your first church?"

"Yes."

"We got missions in my area, all run by the Catholics — Jesuits. They're a special order."

"You a Catholic, James?"

"Call me Jim. No, I'm a Protestant. My wife is a Catholic. She is a Gros Ventre Indian."

"You're married to an Indian? Aren't they savages?"

"She has a better education than most whites in the Territory. She's far from a savage."

"What are you doing way down here, Jim?"

"I'm going to Texas to buy cattle to take back home with me."

"Jim, this is my wife, Percilla, and our child is Mary. We should be making a stop soon. This stage stops every four hours for a short rest and a new team of horses."

"Good. I could use a cup of coffee. I can't take that coffee they make along the Mississippi. It tastes like mud, has a big wad in the bottom of the cup."

"That's French coffee — they make it strong."

The girl on Jim's shoulder woke and jerked away when she found she was sleeping on a stranger's shoulder. Jim said, "It's all right, ma'am."

She just folded her hands on her lap and cast her eyes down.

"That rancher sure can sleep. You'd think he was dead."

"You read the Bible much, Jim?"

"I did when I was younger. I don't even have one now."

"I'll give you a copy, Jim, when we get to a stop. I have a case of them with me."

"I thank you, James. Be good to have something to read. This is about the roughest road I've ever been on."

"We have this gumbo that gets to be a mess when wet, and red dust when dry."

"We got the same stuff in my area, only some red and some gray. Gets wet, sticks to your boots, and you're bigger each step."

It got to mid-day. The stage coach stopped for lunch and a change of team. The lunch wasn't much: a watery stew and stale bread. But there was some good, cool water. The stop lasted only about thirty minutes. When they climbed back in it was the first time the rancher was awake.

"Looks like you could sleep anywhere."

"That I could. Name's Will Rider from near Abilene. This is my wife Michelle. She don't speak English, only French."

"You speak any French?"

"No, but I went to New Orleans for a wife. Got her. She's going to have to learn English."

"She's a very beautiful woman. I'm pleased to meet you," Jim said, taking her hand.

She smiled and said, "*Enchanté*."

"I guess that's good," Jim said. "'*Enchanté* to you."

Michelle laughed.

The rancher said, "You're doing fine, Jim. It means, 'Pleased to meet you.'"

"Will, your wife has that olive skin and green eyes. She's a mixed blood. I don't want to insult you, but my wife is a Gros Ventre Indian."

Michelle started to laugh. In very broken English, she said, "*Gros Ventre* is 'big belly.'"

"Maggie doesn't have a big belly — not yet anyway."

"Yes, Jim, she's what they call Creole. She got a French father and a Negro mother. It makes a good combination. Both parents speak French."

"You telling me you just decide to get married, then go shopping for what you need?"

"It's not that bad. I needed a wife and can give her lots of security. We had some time to get acquainted and had a big church wedding, so we did everything according to propriety. She'll learn English. So, you said you're looking for a herd to take back to Montana?"

"That's true." He wondered if Will saw any difference between shopping for cattle and finding a good wife.

"Maybe I can help you. You can go down along the Mexican border and get half-dead cattle or go a little north and get a herd been culled down a little. How big a herd you want?"

"Oh, about a thousand head."

"You'll get pretty good stock for about five dollars a head. Probably make the trip and only lose fifty-sixty head, but you'll make that up in calves."

"How 'bout a team to help drive them north?"

"That'll be your easy job."

Will Rider had made a lot of money shipping cattle to the troops on both sides during the War and was still shipping cattle to the East. He worried about the cattle surviving the winters in the North, and was interested to know that they did survive, but hay had to be cut and stacked and the animals brought to a sheltered area.

Jim told him how he wanted to move the cattle early, arriving in the spring in Montana, maybe beating some of the calving on the trail. He was thinking he would need horses, wagons, men and equipment.

When they arrived in Fort Worth, Jim decided not to go to San Antonio, but to continue on to Abilene with the rancher and see if it would be a good starting point. He said goodbye to the preacher and his family and changed his ticket. They would stay overnight in Fort Worth and leave early the next morning. Jim told Will that he would see him in the morning, and found a hotel with a bath.

Jim took off the clothes he had been wearing the last four days. He told the hotel clerk to get them washed and back to him soon; then he submerged himself in the tub to soak for the next hour. He put on clean clothes and took a walk around the town. It was a western town, lots of saloons and cowboys. It was also a place for trading horses and cattle.

Jim picked up some ideas on what prices were. Cattle were

going for eight to ten dollars a head, and good horses for a hundred dollars. Maybe Abilene really would be a good place to set up his cattle drive.

How long would the drive take? He figured the distance: a little over 1,500 miles. They should cover twenty miles a day, so it would be seventy-five to eighty days. Almost a three month drive. He would want to be on the trail in mid-February; he should just miss the snow but would still find some high rivers.

Back in the stagecoach the next day, Jim and Will continued their conversation about Jim renting some pasture to start building a herd. Will also told Jim that he could take a crew down and cross the border and steal his own cattle, but it would be better to buy it half-fat. The Mexican cattle were all skinny. This was the second time he told Jim this.

The first person Jim would need was a good foreman. He wished he had brought Little Mac with him. He could be trusted and would be able to work with the trail hands. Well, Little Mac wasn't with him and he would have to make it on his own.

Maggie Wells
c. 1875
Fort Benton, Montana

Lee Roy Wells
c. 1885
St. Peter's Mission

William Wells
c. 1894
Fort Benton, Montana

Emma Wells and Mary Wells
c. 1894
St. Peter's Mission

CHAPTER ELEVEN

The Cattle Drive

W HEN THE STAGE finally arrived in Abilene, Will invited Jim to stay at his ranch. Jim gratefully accepted. At the station they were met by Will's foreman with a wagon and carriage. "Mr. Wells is here to start himself a herd," Will said.

They rode a few good miles to a beautiful valley filled with cattle. Jim was amazed. "You ought to sell me some of yours," he said. "You know how many head you have here?"

"Probably fifty thousand, and I can make a lot more shipping it east. But we'll find you a herd easy."

"What's the name of that river running over there?"

"Called Double Mountain."

"How big a spread you got?"

"I don't know. Direct around fifty thousand acres, plus that much again in grazing land. How's this — what I'll do is lease you a section at ten cents a head, all the water and grazing you need until you start north."

"That sounds more than fair."

"If you want, I'll put the word out you're buying. Fair market value's four to five dollars a head, you brand and control."

"I'm ready, Will."

The wagon pulled up in front of a large house surrounded by many outbuildings. Will had done very well. Jim's room was large and clean and had a view down the valley. That evening after dinner, he worked on a design for a branding iron, "WP," for Wells and Power.

Jim borrowed a horse to ride back into Abilene early the next morning. There he stopped at the blacksmith with his branding iron design. He could have a dozen made by early afternoon. He then went around to the saloons and spread the word that he was looking for a cook, foreman and crew for a drive north to Montana. Later he walked over to the livery stable to see what they had for sale.

"You have any good horses here?"

"You come at the right time, mister. A man just sold me his horse and took the stage east. Damned good horse."

"Let me see him."

It was a strong young bay, chestnut in color. "What are you asking?" Jim said.

"I want one hundred and fifty. That includes all his gear."

"That's too much. Let me see the gear." It was all fairly new, including a beautiful Mexican saddle.

"Why did the man leave?"

"I don't ask. Said he made money on cattle from Mexico. Going east for the easy life."

"I'll give you one hundred and twenty-five dollars."

"It's yours. I'll get the papers. As you can see, no brand. You should put on yours."

Jim paid the man, saddled up and rode off on his new horse,

leading the one he had borrowed. He picked up his branding irons and returned to the ranch.

"Nice animal, Jim," said Will.

"Paid a little much, but I think he is a good horse. Where you think he came from?"

"Probably from across the border. Especially with no brand, good-looking gear, cost a few dollars to have that made. What did you pay?"

"Got the whole mess for a hundred twenty-five."

"Good deal. Just fair horses around here cost seventy-five dollars. That one's worth the money."

Having the ranch as a headquarters would work well for Jim, since everyone knew Will. Just three days after Jim arrived, a rancher came by with a herd of 400. He would sell the whole lot for four dollars a head. Jim and Will went over to check and both felt it was a good deal. The cattle had been brought up from the south — again no brands.

Within a week Jim had been contacted by a Captain MacDougle who wanted the job as foreman. MacDougle had been a captain in the Union Army and was now moving cattle west to east but wanted to try north for a change. He had a head rider named Kid, a cook, and a cook wagon. "Everyone just calls me 'Cap,'" he said. "Got letters from other drivers you can check. I'm honest, hard-working, a good shot, and I can work men."

"What pay do you want?"

"Fifty-five dollars. Found men get forty and the cook thirty-five. We got our own first mounts — you furnish additional mounts."

"This cook any good?"

"He's a Mexican, so lots of beans. Men like his cooking."

Jim liked this man right off. "Cap, you and your men are

hired. I've started the herd and they need to be branded. I'll show you where to set up camp."

"Good deal, Mr. Wells."

"Call me Jim."

They rode out together to a canyon off the main valley where Jim's cattle were grazing. "I'm keeping them here so they won't mix with Will's. I want to put together a herd of a thousand to twelve hundred. Want my brand on all, so Cap, this is your home."

"Looks good. I'll bring the cook wagon and men out here and get started."

Jim's next buy was horses. A herd of around 200 was coming through Abilene. "You want to sell some of your horses?" Jim asked the owner.

"Sure, if you got the money."

"I need about twenty-five."

"Them's all broke and shod, good horses. Seventy-five dollars each, you pick."

"How 'bout seventy, I still pick?"

"Yeah, sounds good."

So Jim, Will, Cap and some of Will's hands helped Jim cut out twenty-five of the better horses. When they were finished, Jim told the owner, "I need a bill of sale for twenty-five horses at seventy dollars — comes to one thousand seven hundred and fifty dollars."

"I've got it right here. Sure you don't want more?"

"No, that should be plenty. You have good horses."

"I raise them myself."

They drove the horses back to the ranch and put them with the cattle. "It looks like you're getting serious, Jim," said Will.

"Yeah, but I still need more cattle and men."

The men and cattle came in, another hundred head of cattle and another man. Within a couple of weeks Jim had eleven hundred head and twelve men. The crew was busy from sunup to sundown, putting the "WP" brand on every piece of livestock.

Jim couldn't thank Will enough for his hospitality, friendship and advice. He was learning a lot about cattle just being around Will's spread, and his cattle were settling down the longer they were in pasture.

"What bull do you think will come out leader of the herd, Cap?" Jim asked.

"That big bull over yonder. Couldn't have come out of Mexico — too big. But must have had good parents. You should keep him for breeding."

"Maybe I could put him together with the buffalo and come up with something new. Big taste like beef and can survive that Montana weather."

"How them buffalo survive without hay cut?"

"They have this big head they use like a plow, only they swing it side to side. They push the snow out of the way down to the grass. You see this big brown mass with icicles hanging all over, you think they're dead, until you get close — ugly animal."

"Still millions of them up there, Jim?"

"No, they're getting killed off fast. The Army figures if they get rid of the buffalo, they can control the Indians."

"Indians don't like the taste of beef."

"Will have to, soon."

Jim was ahead of schedule and didn't want to hit any late snowstorms, but it had been a mild winter. They could always take a break along the trail and end up with fatter cattle at the end of the drive.

If they could do twenty miles a day Jim was told it would take about eighty days. Will helped him with the route. They would travel from Abilene to Amarillo to Denver to Cheyenne to Casper, then to Billings and finally to the Judith. There would be lots of Indians, but he was finding good men and he would be willing to trade beef for passage.

It sure would be good to get on the trail and head home. Jim hoped that things were going well back at the Judith and wished he could be there with Maggie. How he missed her.

Jim took a ride up to the canyon. He saw the campfires of the cowboys, who were eating; over the sound of the grazing, snorting cattle Jim even heard someone singing. Will had told him, "A good cowboy sings to himself, the cows and his friends." The ranch was one beautiful place, this valley with water and grass.

Jim took his horse back to the barn, gave it a good rubdown, and went in to wash for dinner. Dinnertime was still a little rough, since most of the conversation left Will's wife out. There she would sit, proper and beautiful, only taking small amounts of Texas food, which consisted of a lot of meat and beans.

"Will, my herd's starting to look good. Might be pulling out next week."

"Jim, you know you're welcome as long as you want."

"I know that, but I want to get home. But I feel as if you are a good friend and will keep in contact."

"Thank you, Jim."

Jim could feel that Will would be lonesome without a guest.

"One thing, Jim," Will said. "I would like to shoot that Henry you carry. You take good care of it."

"I've had it with me many years. You're welcome any time."

Jim wasn't a drinking man, but he enjoyed Will's after dinner brandy. It came all the way from France. The best stuff Jim had had since leaving San Francisco was whiskey before it was cut down for the Indians.

Jim went into town the next day and bought a dress and some material for Maggie. Then he went and outfitted himself.

One new piece of garb Jim had to get used to was chaps, the seatless riding breeches worn by cowboys. They worked well in this Texas sagebrush, which cut your legs like razors. He also bought himself a set of spurs. He would laugh at himself — he had gone from frontiersman to cowboy. But all pieces had their use, especially the bandanna, the large colored handkerchief worn around the neck to catch the sweat or over the face to keep out the dust. He had used them out in California before.

In the next few days, he was able to pick up another hundred head, so his total was up to 1,200. The branding was moving right along and Cap was able to enlist more men. At last they set the date they would start the drive: the last Saturday in February, 1872.

Jim settled up with Will. "I sure feel like I'm cheating you. All this hospitality, grass and water for my herd, and I give you a hundred and twenty dollars. 'T'ain't right."

"Jim, I told you ten cents a head, that's the deal."

"Could I give you my old Henry?"

"No, I had the pleasure of shooting it."

"Well, we're all ready to pull out on Saturday. Anxious to get home."

"I know that feeling. You have that map I gave you? You should hit Amarillo in about fourteen days. You can re-supply there. Remember, only let half your men in town at a time and always keep on guard. People try to steal your herd every place along the trail."

"Cap seems to know the drive."

"I agree, Cap's a good man as trail boss. Men seem to respect him."

The men checked all the gear and equipment and Jim sent the cook into town with a couple of men to re-supply and ready his cook wagon. Jim gave him one last instruction: "Make sure you bring plenty of coffee."

"*Sí*, Boss."

Friday afternoon, Cap called all the men together for their trail rules. "Men, the rules are easy. First: We try to move the herd twenty miles a day. We start the herd early, start the camp early. Second: we all ride twelve hours a day and split the night guard six and six. Third: No booze. You will get your turns in towns along the trail. Fourth: you can draw on your pay along the trail. Fifth: if you're killed, your share goes to the other men. We hire a new man to replace you. Last but not least, Mr. Wells says you get a bonus if you stick to the whole drive. That's about it. I'm the trail boss, Mr. Wells is the overall boss. Any questions?"

"Yeah," one of the man asked, "How long you figure the whole drive'll take?"

"About eighty days."

"How many head you figure on losing?"

"Mr. Wells figures about a hundred to a hundred and fifty head."

"The last drive I was on going north lost half to Sioux, and half the men," the man said.

"Mr. Wells has been trading with the Indians for a long time. He speaks some of their tongues, so when we see Indians don't fire and let Mr. Wells do the talking. Bunk down early — we start tomorrow."

In the morning, Will came out to say goodbye.

"Jim, good luck," Will said, shaking Jim's hand. "Drop a line and remember us."

"*Au revoir*," Michelle said, giving Jim a quick kiss on each cheek.

"Thanks again for all your help. Come on, boys, let's start moving this herd!"

"Jim, you should ride up front or off to the side. The dust's going to be something terrible."

It wasn't long before the herd started. "Get them cattle moving. They'll be strung out from here to Montana," yelled Cap.

"Goddamn dust's starting to rise already."

As they pulled away from the river, the green grass started to turn brown.

"Cap, how do you feel now?" Jim said, riding up to him.

"I'll feel a lot better when we get a couple of days on the trail. Trail-break the cattle and this green bunch of men."

"If we drive the cattle twenty miles, won't they settle down for the night?"

"Only if nothing spooks them. The Kid's a good scout — he'll find a good place with grass and water for the night. How you holding up?"

"Sure a lot of dust. I'm spitting mud balls."

"That's why you drink coffee at night, to wash the mud down. This is a good-sized herd. Easy to move. You get two-three-four thousand, they string out for miles. This one, you can see both ends. Center's bulging a little, but we'll correct that tomorrow."

"I'll get my first taste of your cook's food tonight."

"He does pretty good, Mr. Wells. We'll start to shoot fresh meat in a couple of days. He can cook anything from rattlesnake to horse."

"He won't have any surprises for me."

The day grew hotter and the dust thicker. Jim wanted to pull off and find a nice stream and soak. He wondered how the men cleaned all that dust off at the end of each day. If it kept building up they wouldn't be able to ride. If he looked out he couldn't see half the men, and those he did see all looked alike.

The first day they made almost twenty-four miles. The campsite was on a river with lots of grass. As soon as the cook wagon pulled into camp, the horses were unhitched and hobbled and a fire started. It wasn't long before the food was cooking. Jim could smell the coffee. He was hungry.

The men were moving the cattle into as small a cluster as possible. Then half the men came into camp, washed and ate steak, beans, biscuits and coffee, as much as they wanted. When they finished, they took fresh mounts and rode off with the herd; then the second group came in, washed and ate. All the men settled around the campfire; after resting they took the second watch.

Jim and Cap finally sat down to eat. "The herd seems a little restless, Cap."

"Always do until, as I said, they're trail-broke."

Jim could hear the men singing to the cattle which seemed to settle them some. Jim sat back and fell asleep. The next thing he heard was the clattering of pots and skillets for breakfast.

"You sure went out, Jim. Sleep good?"

"Sure did, Cap. Don't remember a thing."

Breakfast was bacon, biscuits with gravy made from the grease of the bacon, and coffee. Everyone ate well, knowing they would not eat again until dinner. They would, on this trip, get two types of biscuits: a small, soft one made from leavened dough, or a flat, hard cake made from unleavened dough. The men chewed on these during the day. Having a Mexican cook, this group would also have tortillas, made of unleavened corn meal and cooked on a hot piece of iron and used instead of bread. Jim liked the tortilla; it reminded him of Indian flatbread.

The second day went easy, but the sky was darkening and it looked like a storm was on its way.

"We're lucky — we'll have some rain, but it's too early for sandstorms. Those are the worst."

"Cap, you think that storm'll hit tonight or tomorrow?"

"Probably tomorrow. Looks like it's carrying a lot of water."

That evening the camp was made on a knoll. All the men covered themselves with slickers or oilskin covers to keep out the moisture.

The beans were starting to get to the men. "Never heard so much noise out of a bunch of cowboys," laughed Cap.

"Having a Mexican cook, you'll hear from us the whole trip," answered the Kid.

"I'm married to a Gros Ventre Indian," Jim said. "All the groups have special names. One group's always breaking wind at night, so they got the name 'Night Hawks.' So I guess I'll give you the same name. From now on, this trail crew will be the 'Night Hawks.' You can just say you're practicing your song."

The men got a good laugh out of this, and you could hear them kidding one another.

"Hey, you practicing your song over there?"

"Hear the Night Hawks flying."

"Damn, those birds are loud!"

"Look out, Night Hawk coming."

"That's one rotten bird."

"Thanks, Jim," Cap said. "You put a little humor in the men."

"I'll tell you, Cap, them beans are powerful. Might as well have some humor."

The storm hit right after breakfast the next day. It wasn't long before every inch of Jim's body was soaked. No dust at least. Now it was mud everywhere. Jim could see the wagon having trouble as it sank up to its hubs. The cattle moved slowly as they sank in.

"Don't think we'll make our twenty miles today," Cap yelled to Jim.

"How long's this damned rain going to last, Cap?"

"No telling. Could break, could go on a couple of days."

"Do we have any rivers ahead?"

"No, Jim, not for a few days."

"Good."

But as the day went on, the rain seemed to come down harder. Jim could feel a chill. They kept pushing the herd forward. In the late afternoon they came to a protected area next to a bluff where they stopped for the night. It would be one long, cold, wet night. The dinner was cold leftovers. Men filled their plates and ran trying to find a protected spot before the plate filled with water. Jim, Cap and a couple of men got under the cook wagon, which offered only a little protection. Jim tried to sleep sitting up between the wheel and axle shaft, pulling his oil slicker around him. He must have dozed off.

When Jim woke the sun was coming up and he could smell coffee. He crawled out on his hands and knees, shivering. The men were hanging wet clothes and gear all over the cook wagon. It was the muddiest bunch of cattle and men Jim had ever seen.

"I'm so stiff I'll never get straight again."

"Here, Boss, here's some hot coffee."

"Thanks, Peppy."

"By the way, my name is 'Pepie', not 'Peppy.' The cowboys always say 'Peppy' — not right."

"All right, Pepie. What's your helper's name?"

"Carlos."

"In American, is that Charles?"

"*Sí*,"

The hot food tasted good. The best thing was the coffee. "You sure make this good, Pepie."

"It's Mexican boiled coffee."

He had a big pot, into which he put coffee in a little cloth sack and cooked it over the fire. It was the same way Jim made it, but Pepie's tasted better. "You use something in your coffee, Pepie?"

"*Sí*, Mr. Wells. A little chicory. It comes from New Orleans."

"I hope you got a lot of that chicory stuff."

"Yes, I got a big bag."

The sun came out hot and they could actually watch the land steam. It wasn't long before Jim's buckskin was dry and the mud on the cattle caked, cracked and fell off in big hunks.

The day moved quickly. Jim was going to hate to see the sun go down before his bones warmed. The Kid found them a good campsite, good fuel and water. They had stew for dinner and sat around the campfire.

"Mr. Wells?"

"You're Gus, right?"

"Yes sir. How'd you become a trader in Montana?"

"Well, I was going to make big money in the fur business. But I got sick and was saved by Indians. I got to know their language and started trading. But the furs started slowing down and I wanted to settle down, so I'm moving me a herd."

"Still lots of free land in Montana?"

"It's a big territory and you can still find land. I'm in the southern part — lots of land on the other side of the Missouri River. Still some Indian trouble."

"We should have some Indian trouble on this trip."

"I hope not."

Cap said, "Come on, men, turn in. Got another big day tomorrow. Put the Night Hawks in the bed roll." He put a couple of big logs on the fire.

Things fell into a routine. Pepie was good at providing a variety of meat. When he couldn't find a deer or other wild game, they killed a cow that had gone lame or sick. Jim wanted his men to have good food and lots of it.

On the fifteenth day, the cattle had to swim the Red River. They were now just outside Amarillo. That night Cap laid out the rules.

Half the men would go into town, the other half would move the herd. When the first group came back, the other half would go into town and catch up with the herd. Pepie would go into town with Jim and re-supply. They would catch up with the herd later. All men needing an advance should see Mr. Wells. The group split itself and those going to town headed for the river and a bath, and off they rode.

"That poor town. I wonder how many I'll have to get out of jail tomorrow?"

"I'll tell you one thing, Jim. It will be a quiet group for a couple of days on the trail."

"I hope, Cap, the rest of the trip goes this smooth."

"Still a long way to go. It's easier now with the cattle trail-broke."

Jim did bail one of the hands out of jail the next day. He had been in a fight and broken a table and chair. It cost Jim twenty dollars.

Pepie found everything he needed at the store and had the wagon loaded. Jim paid the clerk and asked Pepie, "Want to stop at the saloon and get a drink?"

"No, Boss, they don't like Mexicans up here. I want to go back to the camp."

"Then let's get moving. You got a family, Pepie?"

"*Sí*, I got a big family in Mexico. But I am not married. Saving my money to buy a ranch in Mexico then get married."

"Sorry I didn't pronounce your name right. Just not used to names down here yet."

"It's all right. You're a good boss, always worrying about your men."

"In Montana, good men are hard to find, and when I get a group as good as this one, I want to take care of them."

"You sure you don't want to stay in town and drink, Boss?"

"No, I'm not much of a drinker. The faster we move this herd, the happier I'll be. I want to get home."

"You married an Indian . . . a Mexican is half Indian, half Spanish."

"Yes, I'm married to a wonderful Indian woman. Sure miss her. She's pregnant with our first child. If it's a boy I'd like to name him Will after the rancher. I'll see what Maggie thinks. If it's a girl, I know she wants to name her Mary. Don't think we'll give them Indian names — too hard. Carlos a relative of yours?"

"*Sí, señor*, I mean mister. Well, he is the son of my brother."

"It's great to hear you speak Spanish, so don't correct yourself. Maybe if I'm lucky I'll pick up a few words."

They caught up with the herd in early evening. They had picked a spot for a night camp and the fire was ready for Pepie to start the evening meal.

"No rest for you." Jim gave Pepie a pat on the back.

The first group of men were back from town, along with the man Jim had retrieved from jail. All looked half sick, but not a one complained; they slipped back into their routine, only eating a light dinner.

"I think they all want to die. The funny thing is when they are out watching the cattle tonight, the smart ones will tie themselves to the saddle. Others won't, and when they can't keep their eyes open, off they fall from the horse. It sure wakes them up."

"Cap, you think we ought to take a day and let them rest?"

"No, Jim. We'll never get there, with a day off after every town. They've been doing this as long as they've been riding."

The next day was routine, even with half the men still in town. "Hope the others get back here by noon," Cap said. "We cross the Canadian River and it's a big one. We need a good crossing. I think I'll ride ahead and check it out."

"Want me to come with you, Cap?"

"No, I'd rather have you stay with the herd, Jim."

"The men will all settle back in. The next big city is Denver. That's over three weeks away."

Jim knew this would be the long part of the trip, from Amarillo to Denver, almost five hundred miles. Maybe twenty-five days if they could keep up the pace. The trail around Amarillo was well-marked, which made it easier for the men to keep the cattle moving.

It was close to noon when the other half of the men rode into camp, yelling and singing. They looked better than the first group did when they returned. Without saying much, they too slipped into their positions along the herd, and things were back to normal.

Early that afternoon they came to the river where Cap and the Kid were waiting for them. "Move the herd upriver 'bout a mile. It's the best place to cross, but the cattle will have to swim. The river's deep on the far side," Cap called to the men.

It was a good-sized river and the water was moving fast. "Put a rope on that lead bull, get him in the water. Come on, put that bastard to the other side," Cap yelled.

The bull was putting up a fight and pulled a horse and rider over backwards. But he made it to the other shore. The other cattle moved in, bellowing in protest, while the men on horses yelled and whipped the cattle with ropes. The cattle hit the current and didn't emerge from the water until they were half a mile downstream. It was good fortune that the river had shallow banks. It took a couple of hours to cross. Jim could hear one of the men shouting, "Don't think we lost a goddamn one."

A few had cuts where a horn had slashed them while thrashing in the river. The cattle moved across much better than buffalo.

They moved the cattle a couple more miles to where the grass was thicker, and set up camp on a small stream. Jim told the men what a good job they did getting the cattle across the river and about how he had watched buffalo cross the Missouri in the spring and how many were killed in that swim. They were all interested in hearing about buffalo, since only a couple had ever seen them. Jim told them how the Indians hunted the buffalo and how herds would be run over a bluff and slaughtered, and how he had seen many killed for just two parts, the tongue and the hump.

It had been a long day and those on the first shift were asleep fast. You could hear the Night Hawks singing.

The trail life was rough. Jim was in the saddle fourteen hours a day. Pepie was up well before dawn to start breakfast, clean up, drive the wagon all day, cook up dinner, clean, then wake early the next day to do the same routine all over again.

Jim didn't think many of his men were saving money. They seemed to live from month to month and spend what they had freely. But talking to them, not one would give up the life. All would say, "Born a cowboy, die a cowboy."

The herd was looking good. Because it was early in the year, grass and water were plentiful. Many of the things Will had told Jim continued through his mind: get rid of the bulls, save the cows, sell old cows. Cattle ranching was going to be something new, but he had his start just getting them there.

The days passed. The only attack they were resisting so far was from the mosquitos. The side away from the wind on a cow would be black with them. All the men had red welts on any exposed skin. "Damn bugs. Big enough you could ride them," said Tex, one of the cowhands. "Won't have enough blood to get to Montana." The mosquitos were thickest when they were near water; when the trail took them away from a river the mosquito population dropped.

"You got mosquitos in Montana, Mr. Wells?" one of the hands asked.

"Not as big as the ones down here in Texas. Also, ours aren't out this early. Still got snow on the ground."

Pepie knew how to control them around the cook fire. He would throw a green log in the fire, causing a lot of smoke. At first the cowhands would complain about it, but as soon as they found out the smoke drove off the mosquitos, the cloud of smoke became the favorite place to sit.

"In Mexico, we don't have mosquitos in our houses because we cook on open fires," Pepie was telling the cowhands.

"You can also rub the leaves of a bay tree on your skin. We did that out in California," Jim said.

"Be careful with bay leaves. Too many crushed leaves give you a headache when you smell them."

"Mr. Wells, you ever cook bay leaves and smell the steam for your cough?" the Kid asked.

"Oh sure. Talk about medicines, the Indians have lots of good ones. Their medicine man has a lot of power. Saved me one time. Pepie, you have a lot of good traditional cures down your way, right?" Jim asked.

"*Sí*, Boss. The white men is always afraid of our medicine. But it works for us."

"Look, Pepie. I got my medicine bag around my neck, given to me by my wife Maggie."

"Know what's in your medicine bag?" Cap asked.

"No, Cap, but if my wife says to wear it, I wear it. I've been in some good Indian fights and I'm still alive."

"You've fought the Indians, Mr. Wells?" one of the hands asked.

"A few times. Once a redhead town woman got scalped. We saved her life. I had to buy a wig off a river boat to give her. It was one ugly wig but she wore it."

"You're kidding us, Mr. Wells."

"No. Maggie treated her with some herbs and grease and the scalp healed, but no hair. She had a big round bald spot. She was one sick lady, but tough. She walked around with a blanket over her head like an old squaw."

"She happy with the wig?"

"It was lucky to even find a wig in Montana," Jim said.

The men laughed.

"You got white men up in your area?"

"We have maybe fifteen at my post. Lots in town and in the mining camps. Then we have the troops. But you can go a long way sometimes and not see a white man. It's still open territory. The cold winters drive most out."

"You plan to stay or make your fortune and move on?"

"Don't know about making a fortune, but I make a living and plan on staying there to raise my family. They can bury me on the banks of the Missouri. I like the life. Maybe some of you will want to stay. I'm going to need some hands."

"I think most of us will wander back and get another herd to move. How come you didn't stay in California?"

"To tell you the truth, too crowded. I don't want to dig for gold, and I love the land. Montana's got it."

Spending the evenings this way on the trail, Jim was amused that the men were so interested in his experiences.

They were seeing a lot of rain on the trail. It seemed to spill at night, giving them most of the day to dry out.

One day the Kid came back from the lead. He had spotted a band of Indians. Jim rode ahead to see if he could communicate with them.

The band was a group that Jim had never seen before. He

counted about thirty-five, including the women and children. It was a poor group; all looked underfed, including the horses. Jim went out to meet the old leader. They both used sign language as best they could. They were asking for food.

"Boss, you want the men to run them off for you?" the Kid asked.

"No. Keep the herd moving. Tell the men to cut out a couple of the older, slower cows and bring them up here to me."

Jim tried to tell the leader what he was planning to do. The old man looked puzzled. Finally he saw two of his men pulling two steers over. Jim took one of the ropes and handed it to the tribe's leader. This brought a big grin to his face and he gestured his thanks to Jim. The rest of the Indians came charging up, startling the two steers; they had a hard time controlling them.

Then, as quick as Jim had ever seen, a young buck ran up and slit the throat of one of the steers and hung onto its head until it dropped. Almost as fast, the group started to skin and cut it up. The other steer was tied to a tree as a fire was started.

Jim rode back to the herd. "How come you gave them those two steers, and not just run them off, Boss?"

"Just think about it. If they sneak into the herd they may start a stampede. We'd lose a lot more than a couple of cows. Also we have friends now, not enemies. It's a cheap toll."

That night the talk of the camp was how the Indians almost ate the cow before it hit the ground. Jim told the men, "We should only fight when necessary."

Jim had seen many stampedes among the buffalo: panic-stricken rushes that nobody could control. He had seen a buffalo trip and fall, while the mass of other bodies tried to get over the carcass; after the herd slowed down, there were hundreds of dead animals littering the plain. Jim would tell the drivers again and again to avoid trouble whenever possible.

In the morning it started to snow. At first the snow melted as soon as it hit the ground, but the flakes began to accumulate as the men finished breakfast. "You men get them cows moving — could be a big storm," Cap yelled. "This is a late snowstorm, but it could be a bad one. Want to get this herd as far as possible before it gets too deep. Damn storm coming from the southwest. That's where we get our worst storms," he said to Jim.

"Cap, if we find a good wooded area we could hole up for a day or two. Let's play it out and hope it's a light one."

The snow continued all morning, and by noon there was a foot and a half on the ground. Jim had never seen snowflakes so big. Fortunately, the snow didn't have much water in it so it wouldn't raise rivers and streams. By early afternoon they decided to stop. The cattle and horses were tired from plowing through the drifts.

"This storm don't look like it's going to let up. Tell the men to get some rest. Make sure the men wipe the sweat off the horses — don't want them to get sick." Cap kept barking out commands. "Pepie, get a big fire going over near the bluff out of the snow. Let's get some hot coffee going."

That night Jim was cold and the snow fell all night long. He coughed a good deal and was happy to see dawn. Two feet of snow had been left on the ground.

"What do you think we should do, Cap, wait for this to melt or push on?"

"Jim, we got to move on. No grass for the herd and they can make their own trail through it. Looks like we're going to have a nice day. Maybe the sun will melt this stuff."

"Too damn cold to melt anything."

"Men, keep your eyes covered and your hat low. You can go blind from the glare. Let's get some hot food and start moving these babies."

It would be another slow day. The cattle at the head of the

herd would push through the snow for a while, then drop back as a new group moved forward. The old lead bull wouldn't give up his position and as the day wore on, Jim didn't think the animal would last. His tongue hung out and he took each step with what looked to be great pain.

"That old bull won't be chasing no cows around the pasture tonight," one of the outriders said to Jim.

"Been watching him all day. Sure is determined. I'd hate to have to eat him. He'd be so tough we couldn't chew him," Jim answered.

"Mr. Wells, we could give him to the Indians. It would take them all year to eat him, if they could."

"I'll tell you, with his determination he'll make it all the way to Montana and still be good for breeding. That's what we all look like up there," Jim laughed, as he rode back toward the chuck wagon.

They pushed hard all day and Jim felt they must have made at least fifteen miles.

Another cold night. The men kept a bonfire roaring. Jim tossed and turned to stay warm. He got up a couple of times to drink hot coffee. "Having trouble sleeping, Jim?" Cap asked.

"I sure am. Montana's worse, but you have time to dig in and get warm. Hope this breaks soon."

The next day was warmer and the snow was melting, which made for mud. Jim didn't care how much mud there was if he could thaw his bones. The herd kept wanting to stop and eat the grass where the snow had melted away. "Keep them moving," someone shouted.

That night it started to rain. "Damn weather can't make up its mind. First dust, then rain, next snow, now back to rain," Jim yelled to Cap.

"Weather's going to get worse the deeper we get into Colorado."

"Maybe I should have stayed in Texas longer."

"No, Jim, we're still making good time. We should be in the Denver area in another ten days. We've only been on the trail twenty-eight. The herd's still in good shape."

"I do appreciate you and the crew. I guess I'm trying to push too hard."

"We all get trail fever when we got families. But remember, you can only push this herd so fast or they fall down and die."

The weather only worsened. Rain, then snow, then rain again. Jim was wet right down to the bone. He found himself coughing more and hoped not to get too sick.

"Mr. Wells, we miss Denver by about forty-five miles. You want to send Pepie in for supplies?" Cap asked Jim.

"Sure, he can leave and catch up on the other side. Means the men will have to cook for themselves for a couple of days. Make sure you send a guard with him."

"Will do. I'll have him leave early tomorrow."

"I'd sure like to go into Denver to get a hot bath."

"It does sound good, Mr. Wells. We're only about five days from Cheyenne. Everyone can raise hell there. The stretch between Amarillo and Cheyenne is the longest without a town."

"Now we'll have to worry about Indians."

"Thought we'd have Indian trouble before now. Guess most of them are still in winter camp. I only worry about Sioux coming out hungry and mean."

"Hope not, the Army should have them under control."

"The Army can't control anything, Mr. Wells."

The weather finally cleared and it was warm, which gave the men a chance to dry out.

Pepie caught up with the herd three days later with a wagon loaded with supplies. "That Denver a big city. I got everything I need, including some good bacon. They asked why we didn't wait until we were in Cheyenne."

"Supplies are limited in Cheyenne, and more expensive. I want to give the crew the best."

The crew was pleased to have bacon for breakfast, pork in their beans, and pork stew. Everyone was also getting restless as they neared Cheyenne. "I figure they'll blow a whole month's wages in one night there," Cap said.

"It seems crazy. They work so hard all month for one night of fun, booze and women. I guess that's the way of cowpunchers," Jim said.

"Mr. Wells, what do you think about us letting the herd rest for a day outside Cheyenne? A day of grazing would be good for them, and also good for the men."

"I think it might be a good idea, all that nice new grass. Let's move the herd to the far side of town."

A day later they found an area to hole up. There was thick grass and water and it was protected, allowing fewer men to guard the herd. The first were quick to head to town. Jim planned to go in early in the morning and get back to the herd by nightfall. The herd was quick to settle in. They acted like they knew they would have a day to rest.

"Cap, you're not going in with the first bunch?"

"No, Boss. I want to make sure the camp's in good shape. I want to give Pepie a day in town, but he doesn't want to go."

"Cap, you know that Mexicans and Indians aren't treated very well. Maybe he'd go in with me tomorrow. I'll ask him."

That night Pepie cooked a special dinner for those still in camp: steaks, fresh biscuits, beans, and even a cake in the Dutch oven.

"Pepie, do you want to go into town with me tomorrow? We'll go in early, come back in the early evening?"

"Mr. Wells, you know I'm not liked in these cow towns."

"You'll be with me — no cowboy'll give you a hard time."

"*Sí*, I would like to go with you."

"Use a horse and extra saddle, no wagon. You know how to ride a horse?"

"*Sí*."

"All right, early tomorrow then."

In Cheyenne Jim again saw what a railroad could do for an area. It wasn't much of a town, but where the railroad passed through there were large holding pens for cattle being shipped east. The town only had one main street. The main store was Herman & Rothschild Stable and Fancy Goods. To Jim's delight he saw the Rollins House, which had a barber and hot baths.

"Pepie, can I treat you to a bath and haircut?"

"Sounds good, *señor*, but do you think they will let me in?"

"We'll soon find out."

Jim and Pepie tied their horses outside the Rollins House and walked in. "What can I do for you, mister?"

"I want a trim, haircut and bath for the two of us."

"Sorry, mister. Whites only in here."

"Mister, he's white as both of us. He's just got a little trail dust."

A man getting a shave abruptly sat up. "You heard the man — whites only."

Jim looked at the man who was climbing out of his chair. He was one of the burliest, ugliest men Jim had seen in a long time.

"Take your Mexican friend and get out," the man said, grabbing Jim by the arm. Without a moment's thought Jim pulled his gun and hit the man sharply across the face. The big man looked at Jim with wild eyes, but didn't say a word and staggered out.

"Mister," the barber started in, "that's one mean man. He ain't done with you."

"Now how 'bout them haircuts and baths?"

"Yes sir. Please, no more trouble in my shop."

"I asked for a little service, not so much talk."

Jim soaked in the tub for over an hour, asking the attendant to bring in more hot water. He could feel the warmth penetrating to his bones. It was the best he had felt in a long time, but Jim's policy was to avoid fighting at all costs, and he was worried about the man in the barber shop. Something had taken possession of him, looking at the man's cruel, ugly face. He had seen that face before, in Fort Benton when he was with Maggie.

When he was finished with his bath, he found the barber again. "How much do we owe you for your services?"

"Two bits each haircut and trim. Fifty cents for the baths each."

"Here's two dollars in case you lost your customer."

"Thank you mister. Be careful."

Jim and Pepie walked down the street past the saloon. Jim looked in and saw Cap and some of the boys. "Come on, Pepie. Buy you a little 'rock gut.' I could use some myself."

Cap and the boys greeted Jim and Pepie.

"Hi boys! Buy you a round?"

"Thanks, Boss."

Then Jim looked across the saloon and saw the big, ugly man sitting on a table with two other rough-looking cowboys. Suddenly his plans to drink and relax didn't sound so good.

"Don't like this place. Going to buy some goods and have dinner," Jim said to Cap.

"You the one that hit that ugly thing in the head, Boss? He's madder than hell. He's been yelling since he came in."

"Just showed him some manners. Come on, Pepie. Let's get those supplies, and get back to camp."

At dinner, which was some cut of beef in a rancid sauce, Jim said to Pepie, "Your cooking's much better. Too damn much grease in this food."

"Thank you, *señor*."

When they were walking out, Jim saw his new enemy coming across the street with two friends. They were laughing and walking with the swagger of men who had been drinking. The man called, "Hey, you little man with that Mexican. You going out of town feet first."

Jim could see people running in all directions.

"You heard me, little man. No one hits me and lives."

Jim knew this might be his last moment and he said a quick prayer to see Maggie again. He looked the man square in the eyes. "For a big fellow, you still need help."

At that very instant one of the men went for his gun, but even faster, Jim drew and fired, hitting the gunfighter in the shoulder. The shoulder seemed to explode, almost tearing off.

"The next one will be between the eyes, either of you." Jim said, his heart racing. "Now get your friend and back off."

The big man was standing white-faced with his mouth open. He started to speak. "You'll be sorry for this."

Jim looked him in the eyes. "You big dumb ox. Not smart enough to know when to quit. I told you the next one is between the eyes for you — you hear?" He turned and walked off. "Come on, Pepie. Let's head back to camp."

Riding back to camp on their horses, Jim began to gulp. Pepie said, "I didn't know you were such a good shot, Boss."

Jim said, "Neither did I, Pepie."

The herd was scattered when they returned and Jim was worried. He felt there could be more trouble. Cap had left the Kid in charge.

"Kid, I had a little trouble in town. I think you ought to pull the herd in and post a couple of guards."

"Sure, Boss."

A few hours later a group of Jim's cowboys, led by Cap, came riding back into camp. "Boss, you sure raised hell in town today. You're the talk of the town. Seems nobody ever took down that moose before, and his sidekick is one of the fastest guns."

"Cap, it worries me so I asked the Kid to tighten up the herd and post extra guards."

"Probably a good idea. When you pick fights you sure pick big men."

"Big men are big targets."

"Cap, tell the men going into town to take it easy. We need everyone tomorrow to get this herd moving again."

"I wouldn't make a shadow from that campfire — makes a good target."

"You're sure jumpy, Mr. Wells."

"I just don't trust that big man. He's crazy."

Jim found himself waking all through the night, hoping for no more trouble. But he woke to rifle fire and the unmistakable rumble of the herd starting to stampede. "Men, to your feet. Watch out for gunfire."

Jim rode hard, trying to cut off the lead cattle. The moon was casting enough light to see the ground ahead of him and it looked like the herd was heading for a box canyon. Soon he saw the lead cattle trying to climb the canyon wall, some falling back to be crushed. How many steers would he lose tonight, he wondered.

They would have to wait until sunrise to find out the total damage. The rest of the night was long and cold. The moon dropped and the cattle settled down in the box canyon. As soon as there was enough light, Jim and the Kid started to circle the cattle. Jim counted about twenty carcasses right off. Others had wounds from horns and hooves.

"Damn, look at that mess, Boss."

"It could have been worse, especially if it had been a cliff instead of a canyon."

"They must have run seven or eight miles. Looks like we're going to lose another half a day."

"Tell the men, Kid. Kill all cattle with broken legs or bad wounds. Keep count. Pick up strays."

After the order had been given they started back for camp. Jim was sure who had started the stampede, and if he ever saw that man again he would do more than pistol-whip him.

Just after dawn, as they rode back to the camp, Jim saw a body over near a tree. "Kid, look." It was one of his hands, Charlie. Not far away was another body, that of the big man. "Looks like Charlie got a shot off when he was going down."

"Look, Boss. He was shot in the back."

"Yeah, but he put one between the eyes of that guy. Let's get the men to bring them in." When they arrived in camp, Pepie had breakfast ready and the men who were in town had just gotten back.

It was almost noon when the herd made it back. "Lost thirty-three head, counting those we can't find in the bush. Seventeen killed outright, then we shot the rest. We're still short six we can't find."

"Let's bury Charlie and get the herd on the move."

A grave was dug for both men. Cap led a prayer. "Cap, you get that herd on the trail. I'll go back to town and tell the sheriff what happened," Jim said. He felt heavy and grim.

"Just keep coming north, Boss, and you'll find us. Want any boys to go with you?"

"No."

Jim mounted and headed back to the sheriff's office. "Good afternoon. Sheriff around?"

"No," the deputy replied. "He's at the hotel for lunch."

"Thank you. I'll try to catch him." Jim turned and headed for the hotel. As he entered he could see the sheriff by himself eating lunch.

"Sheriff."

"Yes, Mr. Wells. What brings you back to town? I thought you'd be gone."

"Thought I would be too, but I had some trouble last night. The herd was stampeded, and two men were killed."

"Who?"

"That big fellow I gun-whipped, and one of my boys, Charlie, shot in the back."

"So what do you want me to do?"

"Sheriff, I wanted it reported to you. Tell those other guys to stay away or we shoot first."

"Mr. Wells, I tell you, Nat Buck's no loss, and you're welcome to shoot all his friends. Where did you bury him?"

"About fifteen miles out of town along the main cattle trail. Marked it good."

"How much cattle you lose?"

"They ran seven, eight miles up a box canyon. Some killed each other, others we had to shoot. All told, thirty-three."

"I'm real sorry about your man. I'll tell that gang you're looking for them. Should make them look over their shoulders for a while, enough time for you to get up the trail."

"Thanks, Sheriff."

"You better get back to your herd. There's another snowstorm coming."

"Thanks for that good news. If you're ever up to the Judith River, stop by."

"Thanks, Mr. Wells. Good luck."

As he rode north along the trail, Jim could feel the weather changing. The wind was coming from the west, growing cold. Jim didn't catch the herd by nightfall so he decided to find a good place to pull up by himself. One thing he didn't have was food, but it wouldn't hurt him to go without for a day.

He found a coulee that had a good overhang. He hobbled his horse, started a fire and gathered enough wood to last the night. As the fire flickered against the sky he thought about how he had started the fight with the man and how Charlie had died for it. He said some prayers and slept until dawn.

He awoke cold and damp. It had snowed almost a foot, which would make for poor riding. The snow didn't let up and it was hard to see where he was going. At least he could follow the trees that had been barked by the cattle.

It was late afternoon when he finally spotted the old chuck and supply wagon, slowly rolling along. "Welcome back!" Pepie yelled. "You bring the snow with you."

"Hope not. Where's Cap?"

"Don't know, Boss, maybe at point trying to push the cattle."

Jim moved around the herd. He could see the men on their horses over the cattle but couldn't make out any faces. He finally found Cap and some of the men trying to locate a site for the night.

"Boss, it looks like we're going to be here a couple of days. We gotta let this thing blow over. Good protection here for cattle."

Pepie had found a sheltered site and already had a big fire going and coffee brewing. "Boss, want coffee?"

"Sure do." The hot coffee and warm fire felt good. He was really feeling his hunger.

"Pepie, you have any leftover biscuits from breakfast?"

"*Sí*. Frozen."

"That's no problem. I'll dunk them in my coffee. That makes them soft." The biscuits tasted good. He didn't realize how hungry he was.

That night the camp settled in for a long storm. Pepie made lots of stew and coffee, so the men could ride in and warm up anytime.

Cap was right — this storm was going to dump a lot of snow and they would be here a couple of days. If they could just stay warm.

The storm blew the whole next day. Not that much snow fell but the wind made huge snowdrifts. The third day, the sun came out bright and the wind was gone. The reflection from the snow was warming.

"Remember, men, keep those eyes covered. We don't want you going blind," Cap gave the orders. "Let's move these cattle. This stuff should melt fast this time of year."

It was warm enough that Jim took his heavy buffalo coat off and let the heat get to his bones. By early afternoon the herd was moving and the snow had melted away from some patches of ground. But as the sun started to set it grew cold again and Jim could hear the ground freezing and cracking under his horse's hooves.

Tomorrow they would cross the Lodgepole River, which had swelled with this new snow. "Want to hit that river first thing in the morning. It'll give us all day to dry," Cap explained to the men. "Hope the sun is out."

At first light, the herd was pushed into the river. The current was moving faster than expected, sweeping the cattle downriver. "Men, get across and get them cattle back into a herd," Cap yelled.

Jim's horse entered the water and started to swim. The cold water hit Jim and he lost his breath. "God damn this is cold!" he heard the men yell. Jim could see cattle slipping off the far side, trying to get a foothold on the frozen bank.

"Keep pushing them, get them up that bank!"

Jim's horse hit the far bank, slipped once, then was able to climb out. "Thank God that river's not deeper or faster or this beef would be back in Texas," Jim yelled to Cap.

"We shouldn't lose any, but we'll be cold for a while."

Jim watched as the men got the cattle back on the trail. He looked back and saw the cook wagon floating across.

"Should be able to make our miles today, Boss. The snow packed down overnight."

"Sounds good, Cap. I'm all for getting out of this area."

By noon the sun and its reflection had warmed Jim and the snow was melting. The herd was moving at a good pace. Jim thought, "Can't relax or something'll go wrong." He was trying to figure out how long they had been on the trail. As close as he could figure, forty-two days. If things continued at this good pace, it would be another forty days. He figured he had only lost four or five days so far.

The rest of that day went well. As the sun set the ground started to freeze. The Kid had again found them a good place to camp for the night. During supper Cap talked to Jim.

"Will be passing Chugwater tomorrow. It's got a small saloon — may have some lost hands. We could use a few to make up for losing Charlie. And we're entering Indian country now anyway."

"Cap, you make the choice — you're the trail boss. I still worry, with my luck."

The next day was an easy one. Cap took a couple of men and headed for town to try and find more hands.

It was a nice camp. Jim took his supper and went down by the river. It was a wide river, but shallow and clear. The wind was cold and he could see the slow-moving sections of the water starting to freeze. At least only his boots would get wet tomorrow.

The camp settled down for the night and Jim went right to sleep.

In the morning, Cap was back with three new men. He brought them over to Jim. "Boss, this is Jimmy John. He's a half-breed — he knows the country."

Jim shook his hand. "Welcome."

"This is Whiskers. He's a little old but they say he's good with gun and horse." The older man grinned through the thickest beard Jim had ever seen.

"Got to be good to live as long as I have out here," he said, reaching out for Jim's hand.

"Welcome, Whiskers and Jimmy John."

"You say, Boss, you're from the Judith Musselshell area? I got a friend from my mining days up in that area — called Mac — Young Mac, no, Little Mac. Know him?"

"Sure do. He works for me. He's running my trading post. Sure a good man. You'll see him at the end of the drive."

The third was a buffalo soldier who had left the Army in Arizona. He was the first black man some of them had ever seen.

"And here's Tad. Good horseman and shot and works hard."

"Welcome Tad, always use a good man."

Cap said, "I'll introduce you to the rest of the men. Get your positions and get this herd moving."

"Cap, I like those men. You did good," Jim said.

"They were the only men within two hundred miles."

The men accepted the three newcomers, and Jim's worries about how they would take to Jimmy John and Tad were soon over.

Early the next morning, they pushed the herd across the Chugwater River again. It was cold, swift and mean from the fresh run off. "One hell of a way to start off a day — cold and wet," Jim yelled to Cap.

"Talked a little last night to old Whiskers. He knows the trail north pretty good. Could be of some help to us."

"That's good. The country could get rough the farther north we go."

They had to cross two more rivers that day, one around noon called the Laramie and one just before camp, the North Laramie.

"Hope that cook gets a big fire going so we can dry some of this gear out."

"Yeah, Boss, but you ain't seen nothing. The big one's coming up in a couple of days — the Platte River. Whiskers said we should spend some time finding a good crossing, or we could lose cattle."

"Thanks Cap. We'll send him and the Kid ahead tomorrow."

That evening Jim and Whiskers got to talking about Montana and some of the friends they had in common. Whiskers had met Father Giorda in the mining camp. Jim asked him why he was now so far south. He said he was a scout for the Army but didn't like the way the Army was treating the Indians. He left the Army at Fort Fetterman. He got as far as Chugwater and was snowed in for the winter. He made money shooting game for anyone with money.

Whiskers said Jim's drive was the first of the season, and much earlier than most, since they were still having snowstorms. Jim told him he wanted to get back to see his wife, who was soon to have their first child.

Early the next morning, Whiskers and the Kid rode off to check out the river. The rest of the crew prodded the herd along. The area they were passing was known as Medicine Bow, a rich forested area that was sacred to the Indians who had lived in the region. Now only some stray bands of Sioux were around. It was some of the most beautiful country Jim had ever seen.

The sun returned to make it a warmer day. Jim thought he

must be part reptile. He didn't function too well in the cold, but as soon as he found his warm rock and could take in a few rays of sun, he was functioning again.

Jim kept wondering if he had started this cattle drive too early. But the cattle still looked healthy. They were able to find enough grass between snow patches and that last stop outside Cheyenne had fattened them some. And the grass should hold up since they were the first herd to cross since the winter. He knew he was committed and over halfway home. Home — that word sounded good. He wondered how Maggie was feeling.

Jim rode up on a hill and got a view of the Platte. They would be following it until they found a crossing around Fort Fetterman. It was a big river, but not as big as the Missouri. When Jim rode into camp, Pepie had the fire going and the evening meal started. Jim was hungry. Pepie always put on a good feast, even if Jim wasn't always sure what he was eating. It was better sometimes not knowing. Jim took his plate and sat over by the fire. As he sat down, Whiskers came over. "Mind if I sit down with you?"

"No, no, Whiskers. Lots of room on this log."

"The Indians call this area Medicine Bow — it's sacred to them. The Army ran the Indians off. But they still come back. Like taking a man's church from him."

"What kind of Indians still around here?"

"Sioux are still the main ones. The Army still can't control them. It's their land, but the U.S. Government says 'No.'"

"Whiskers, do you think Indians are going to hit us?"

"Well, Boss, it's been a long cold winter. Hungry men will do anything for food. The men said you gave cattle to some Indians a while back?"

"Yeah. Forestall them stampeding our herd."

"You'll be willing to give more cattle to Indians?"

"Sure, if it saves men and cattle."

"You're a good man, Mr. Wells. Not many would go around a fight."

"I'll tell you something, Whiskers. I was sick and hungry, and some Indians saved my life. I'm married to a Gros Ventre. I'm willing to work with them. "

The country was rough and beautiful. The cattle were eating enough grass so the trail was not taking off their fat. "If only those late snowstorms would hold off," Jim thought.

The next couple of days became routine: up early, eat on the trail, dinner and turn in for the night. It was early evening when they could see the fort across the river. "Cross tomorrow, Mr. Wells," Cap said.

"Any men going over to the fort tonight?"

Whiskers said, "It's a dry fort. No night life, no fun."

"Sure like to get a couple more men for the rest of the drive. If you go into the fort you can check," Jim said.

The next morning was clear. The river was high and cold. The men had found a good crossing just a couple of miles up from the fort. The cattle were gathered on the bank, ready for the push by the men. "Let's get this herd across," Jim yelled.

At this command the big mass of animals started for the river. Some of the men were already across the river waiting for the first cattle. The cattle would spread over a mile and a half from floating downstream.

It was time for Jim to hit the water. It went over his saddle and then over his waist. His gun, hanging around his neck, was hitting him in the chest. "Goddamned water is cold!" he let out a yell. But no one could hear him over the noise of cattle and men. He was only in the water for fifteen to twenty minutes, but it felt like hours.

The bank was steep but had been knocked down by the first cattle coming out of the river. As he came up the bank, he heard one of the men yelling, "Hey Boss, I froze my balls off!" Jim laughed, but he was cold.

As he got to the top of the bank he could see the chuck wagon starting to float. It was a fight, wagon against water, horse against wagon and water. "Just keep it moving," he thought.

Jim was lucky — in another couple of weeks the water would really be high — so a little ice bath was worth it.

His men were riding up and down the bank, moving the cattle back into a herd. By the time he gathered them back together, they would only be about half a mile outside the fort. "I'm going ahead to warn the fort we're coming," Jim told a couple of the men. "Set up camp just outside. See you there."

Fort Fetterman was like all the other forts that sat on a river bank: small stockade, a few buildings outside the fort. But it did look like they had experienced a hard winter. The stockade gates were open; in fact, it looked like they couldn't close them if they had to.

Inside the stockade Jim could see the barracks and mess hall, and he finally located the headquarters office. He rode over, dismounted, tied his horse to the hitching post, and knocked on the door. He heard a voice yell, "Enter."

A young man in uniform was sitting at a desk. "Is your commander in, son?" Jim asked.

"No sir, but I will get him for you. Coffee, sir?"

"Please. I'm still a little wet from my swim."

"Please sit, sir. I'll get the captain."

The young private left and Jim sat down near the stove. The coffee sure tasted good, and the fire felt even better.

It was about twenty minutes before the private returned with the captain. "Sorry, sir, for making you wait, but I had to get the troops ready for the day. I'm Captain Hill," he said as he extended his hand to Jim.

"Jim Wells. I'm moving a herd to Montana."

"We knew you were coming for about a week. We thought you might stay on the other side of the river and go west. Welcome. Have you had breakfast, Mr. Wells? We could go over to the mess hall?"

"Sounds good to me, Captain. My name's Jim." As they walked across the compound, Jim said, "Looks like you had a rough winter."

"It's hard to get supplies way out here. Wagons won't come for another month. We eat lots of wild game and salted and dried food."

"You still have good coffee, Captain."

"We make coffee the good old-fashioned way: we boil it, and put in an eggshell if we have one."

"Priest who married me made it that way too. Why eggshell?"

"Makes the grounds drop to the bottom, don't know why."

They moved into the mess hall. A few men were gathered around a stove trying to keep warm.

"Men," the captain roared, "this is Jim Wells, moving a herd of cattle up to Montana. Two meals, lots of coffee."

"Yes sir," was the response.

"Sit down, Jim. They'll bring over our food in a minute. It won't be much but it'll be hot. Probably antelope and biscuits. Be sure to put the biscuits in your coffee — they're so hard we use them for shot in our cannon."

Jim laughed. "If you got lots of coffee, I'd like to buy some."

"If you sell me some of your beef."

"All right. How many head you think you want?" asked Jim.

"Maybe thirty or forty. That'll hold us until supplies come. We pay top dollar. We could use some good beef," the captain went on.

"You care if it's bull meat or not?" Jim asked. "Most of our ladies got calves in 'em, we hope. They'll hold off dropping until we get to Montana."

"Bull will do, as long as they're not too tough. Mind if I look at your herd?"

"They'll be outside your fort in a couple of hours. Say, Captain, how's your Indian problem 'round here?" Jim asked.

"It's been a quiet winter, but you're heading into Sioux country. We kill their buffalo, push them onto bad ground, don't give them what we promised. It makes me sick. I hate them no-good political Indian agents. Don't get me started, Jim, or they'll make me a private."

"Sounds like you have some feeling for the Indians. You know, I'm married to a Gros Ventre up near Fort Benton — got my first young one on the way," Jim said.

"You need to be a tough man, Jim, to try that. I'm doing my time to get a job back East in Washington."

"I've got my trading post and am getting ready to start some cattle. I love it out here," Jim went on.

The food came and, as Jim expected, the only thing good was the coffee. The meat was antelope that had been run to death and could be used for bottoms in his boots. The biscuits were so hard the coffee wouldn't even soak in.

"Captain," Jim started in, "how 'bout you eat with me tonight? We have a damn good cook — some special supplies — you can take a look at my cattle."

"Sounds good, Jim. Be out early."

Jim thanked the captain for the meal. They shook hands and Jim mounted his horse. He could see his herd in the distance and rode out to meet it.

"Put the herd in that nice grassy area. It'll be easy to push out early tomorrow," Jim yelled. He could see the chuck wagon way back, so he rode toward it. "Pepie," Jim called, "make some of those tasty beans and good biscuits. We're going to have a couple of guests tonight. They haven't eaten anything good in months. We'll probably be selling some of our cattle to the Army."

"*Sí*, Boss. I'll set up the wagon early."

Captain Hill came out to the herd later with a few men. He waved at Jim and rode off into the center of the cattle. Jim settled back in the saddle. He knew the captain would be impressed and it would be a good way to get rid of some of the young bulls. The captain and his men came out of the herd about an hour later and rode over to Jim.

"Ready to do business, Jim?" the captain said.

"Sure, Captain. Let's take care of it before we eat."

"Your cattle look good. Don't look like they've been on the trail as long as they have. Tell you what I can do. I'll take thirty head, or forty if you can spare them. I'll give you fifty dollars a head, which is high, but we need beef."

"Hey, Kid," Jim yelled, "take the captain's men out and cut out forty head of bulls, or cows with no calves in them."

"Will do, Boss."

"That was easy," Captain Hill said. "You give me a bill of sale and I have your money here."

Jim wrote up a bill of sale for the captain. "You know, I could make more money selling cattle on the trail than raising it in Montana."

"This is well spent. Keep my troops happy."

"Captain, I almost forgot the last part of our bargain. You going to throw some coffee in?"

"I sure will, Jim. We'll send it out to you."

Jim laughed as the men tried to separate the cattle and the cattle immediately returned to the herd. "You got to put a rope on them troopers," Jim yelled. "You want that old lead bull, Captain?"

"No, thank you. Indians wouldn't even try to eat him. You pull out early tomorrow, Jim?"

"Yeah. I want to keep moving. You know where I might get a couple of good men for the rest of the drive?"

"Try the trading post. A couple of brothers — name's Martin — have been hanging around all winter. Got their own horses and guns. It's worth a try."

"Thanks, Captain. I'll go back with you after we eat. Bring your men over, my boys will watch your cattle."

Pepie outdid himself with steak, beans and fresh biscuits. "Damn, that man can cook. Does he want to join the Army?" Hill remarked. "You have the same food, but our cook destroys it," he went on.

"We do eat well," Jim said. "We bring our own beef with us. And Pepie comes up with some stuff that tastes good, and I don't ask where he gets it."

"Jim, you have some beans to spare?" Hill asked.

"I tell you what. I'll give you a hundred pounds in trade for coffee. I won't charge extra for any bugs you find."

Jim and Hill started back. The soldiers were not cowboys and were having a rough time. When they reached the fort, Jim told the captain it was a pleasure doing business with him and if he ever got to Montana, to look him up.

Jim headed for the trading post. It wasn't much, with fewer supplies than Jim had ever seen at a post. It looked like a few men lived there and didn't move far from the stove. "Got a couple of men named Martin here?" Jim asked.

"Yeah, over here." The two young fellows looked like it had been a hard winter. They were dirty, looked half-starved, and wore ragged clothes.

"Looking for men who want to go north to Montana. You get food, a fair wage and extra mounts. Need to know how to use guns," Jim said. He saw sparks jump into their young eyes.

"We were out in Texas running cattle for a big ranch. We thought we could make money in hides. We stuck it out here all winter and made a little money shooting game for the fort. We ride, shoot good and work hard."

"I'll hire you. If you're no good, I'll leave you on the trail. Name's Jim Wells. I'm moving Texas cattle to Montana."

"I'm Jim, and this is my brother John."

"That's funny. I'm Jim and I have a brother named John. Say we call you Little Jim?"

"You can call me anything as long as you give me a job."

"You got it. Get your gear and come with me."

Jim could hear a loud shout of joy coming from inside the post. He hadn't walked a few feet when Little Jim and John appeared at his side.

"Them pretty sick-looking horses you got. Have the man at camp get you new mounts, and let yours run and feed for a while," Jim said.

All the way out to camp, Jim could feel the excitement coming out of the two young men. Jim felt he had made a good choice. When they reached camp, Jim took them over to Pepie. "Pepie, this is Little Jim and John. Can you feed them?"

"Sure can, Boss."

Jim saw Cap having a cup of coffee. "I found you a couple more men. They're yours now — give them their jobs. You done good moving the herd around today. Thanks, Cap."

"Thanks, Boss."

Jim could see the new men talking to the Kid, so he walked over to Pepie. "Got any coffee?"

"Coffee, Boss? I got coffee — half a wagon of coffee. The Army just kept unloading coffee."

"What do you think of the new men?"

"Good men, Boss, but they eat like they never had food before. I'll have to cook twice as much."

"Pepie, let's get the men down. I want to start early tomorrow."

Jim watched the new men with their old blankets. "Pepie, get a couple of bedrolls out of the wagon and give them to the new men. Also a couple extra coats."

As soon as the sun went down it was cold. Jim just couldn't keep warm.

Everyone was up before dawn and fed a steak, biscuits and coffee. All put a few biscuits into their pockets, knowing that this was the meal until dinner. Next to the biscuits was a pile of jerky. Every cowboy had jerky in his pocket with his biscuits.

"Let's get them cows moving," Cap yelled. "They had a rest and we can make some miles today."

They were making good time. Jim noticed a mountain off to his right, and it was growing. It looked like it came out of nowhere.

"You climb that mountain, Cap, you'd be on top of the world. Ever see something like that before?"

"No, Boss, but we sure have some good grassland out here. Good night grazing, keep the fat on the cattle."

Jim was amazed by the mountain. He hoped they had a moon so he could see it at night. If they could push for three days they should reach the Powder River, and after another four or five days they would be in Montana Territory. This had been a long trip and with Little Jim and John around, Jim realized how much he missed his brother. He laughed to himself thinking how much moaning and groaning there would have been with John on the cattle drive. He hoped his brother was nice and warm in California somewhere.

The next few days were uneventful. As they moved toward the Powder River, Jim was not looking forward to another swim. "Well, Cap, should hit that Powder River tomorrow," Jim said.

"Yeah, Boss. Also starting to see signs of Indians."

"Tell the men to be on the lookout, but no shooting."

The same plan was used the next day to move the herd across: start upstream a couple of miles, let the herd swim down and over, keep hands along the river to push the herd back together again.

"Even crossing the river, we made good time. We must have got damn near twenty-five miles today," the Kid told Jim.

"Got another river tomorrow, but it doesn't look as bad," Jim said.

Early the next morning they crossed the Crazy Woman River. "That's enough rivers for a few days," Jim said.

"Sorry, Boss, we have another coming up again tomorrow," said Cap.

The next morning Cap woke Jim. "Got some bad news, Boss. A couple of cows dropped calves last night."

"We had to expect that. Tell the men that the calves that can't keep up, put in the cook wagon or carry on a saddle. If there's too many, we'll have to slow down. If the cows have trouble giving birth, tell the men to help."

When they hit the Clear River, Jim saw the new calves testing the water with their hooves. But they seemed to be strong and kept up with the herd. Another couple of days and they would be at Fort Sheridan.

That morning they saw a band of Sioux Indians off to the east. "Can't see them giving us trouble this close to Fort Sheridan," Jim said. "Cut out about ten of them bulls and push them off toward the right," Jim commanded.

Jim could see his men following his command. Some had to be roped and pulled, but soon the small band of cattle was running off from the herd. In only moments, Jim could see a band of about fifty Sioux descending on the cattle. The battle was short.

"I think that will give us a couple of days," Jim said.

At Fort Sheridan Jim did some trading and sold a few more cattle to some beef-starved soldiers. He was told that he would be traveling into Crow country and that a few cattle may not buy his passage; it seemed he had been very lucky. A new general was out West. He was out to put all the Indians on reservations and had stopped his campaign in the winter of 1870-71. But Indians from Fort Sheridan north were not too happy. Jim hoped he would get back to the Judith before all hell broke loose.

Two days later they crossed the Little Big Horn River. The weather was warming and his herd was increasing each day as more and more cows started to calve.

Two days after crossing the Little Big Horn, Jim and his herd found themselves in the middle of one of the largest Crow encampments Jim had seen in years. He played it bold and went looking for the chief as if he were a trader.

The Crow chief welcomed Jim and he was invited to dinner. To Jim's surprise, the chief knew of Jim and his trading post at the Judith. Jim also knew that the Crow and Gros Ventre were enemies. Jim was told that Sitting Bull was trying to unite the tribes against the Bluecoats. The Sioux, Shoshone and Crow were uniting but not staying together.

Jim told the chief all he wanted was to be able to pass through the Crow country in peace, and he would be willing to trade cattle and coffee. The chief wanted a hundred head of cattle. Jim said twenty-five. They settled for fifty plus about 300 pounds of coffee.

Jim told his men to cut out weaker or sick cattle for the camp, then get the rest of the cattle on the move. He had Pepie stack the coffee outside the chief's lodge. "See, Pepie," Jim said, "I told you all that coffee would come in handy. It may have just paid for our lives."

It took another five days to get out of the Crow territory. In another week it would be the first of May and Jim would be home. As soon as they found the Judith he could leave the men and ride on alone.

That evening he talked to the men around the campfire. He told them that they were on the last leg of the trip and that any of them that wanted to could stay on at the Judith.

Two days later, Jim left the herd under the command of Cap and the Kid and headed up the Judith. If he rode hard he could make it in a day, and he did.

Maggie heard the shouts of some of the men and came to the trading post door. Seeing Jim, she burst into tears and ran toward him. Jim jumped off his horse, carefully picking Maggie up in his arms. "Maggie," Jim said, "you're as big as our trading post." Jim kissed her and carried her back inside.

Just then, Little Mac came out from the barn to greet Jim. "You made it," he exclaimed, grasping Jim's arm.

"Been a long trip, Mac, but I got one great herd."

"Where is it?"

"About three days down the Judith. I wanted to get home."

"It's a good thing. Lots of Indian trouble. Army's been moving in troops."

Jim took a bath and shaved, while Maggie put out some new buckskins for him. "I look and feel like a new man," Jim said.

Maggie prepared a big meal for Jim. After dinner, Jim sat at the table with Maggie and Little Mac. He talked about his long trip down the river, then overland to Texas, then the long drive home. They were all thankful and amazed that Jim had made it safely.

When they finally retired it was so good for Jim to have Maggie next to him in bed. It was the first time in months he had been warm. He thought how much he loved Maggie. She was such a great and wonderful woman. He was so lucky.

He kissed her and held her close to him. "Maggie, I do love you."

"I love you too, Jim."

CHAPTER TWELVE

Home at the Judith

MAGGIE WOKE JIM AT DAWN and by sunrise showed him the improvements that had been made around the post while he was away. There was a new pump, bringing up water from the river. There was a new barn for hay and several new cabins built for extra help. Jim was impressed. Then Maggie showed Jim the crib she had asked Little Mac to build and the quilt she and Blue Sky had sewn for the baby. Jim thought things looked better than ever.

Later Jim met up with Little Mac. "You did a great job while I was gone. You'll like the men I found in Texas — think some will stay. Still can't believe we had so little trouble from the Indians. They all look so tired and hungry."

"We're in the middle here, Jim. More trouble in the Dakotas and west. But the soldiers are starting to push the Gros Ventres too."

"Today we need to start the pens and cut hay. The new men are good cowboys, so I'll hire cutters and fence builders. Soon as

I get the cattle settled, I'll go see Power in Fort Benton. Should be a busy summer here — first boat in the next couple of weeks."

Jim spent the next two days relaxing and enjoying his home. He looked over all the equipment and construction, met with all the hands, and followed Maggie everywhere she went. He knew that once the cattle arrived he would be hard at work again. Late in the afternoon the second day, Cap rode into the post.

"This is a beautiful spot," Cap greeted Jim. "I can see why you settled here, and why you were so eager to get back." Gradually some of the other men trickled in, followed by the cook wagon and Pepie. Jim proudly introduced everyone to Maggie.

"We've heard an awful lot about you," Cap said, shaking her hand.

"*Sí*, the Boss talked about you every day, I kept count."

Maggie laughed and cooked a big dinner for the crew that night, and Pepie was at her side helping.

"Damn that was good," the Kid said.

"One thing, Kid," Jim started in, "you always get a full stomach at this post. Lots of good game around here."

The next few weeks were busy. Pens, a new bunk house, and a cook house and cabin for Pepie were started. Pepie seemed to have a sweet eye for Blue Sky.

By the middle of June the cabin which Jim and Maggie lived in was cleaned and made ready for the baby. Jim was told he had to move out at this time. Blue Sky gave Maggie her traditional Gros Ventre instructions: if she had to change sides while lying in bed, she must sit up first. She must not roll over, or the cord would wrap around the baby's head. When she went in and out of the house, she must go through the door quickly, so her baby would come quickly. She must never back through the door, because it would make the baby come out the wrong way.

Blue Sky had also put a crossbar in the house for Maggie. Maggie would assume a kneeling position during the birth and grasp the crossbar. A woman would never lie down while giving birth unless she was so weak she couldn't help herself.

Early on June 20, 1871, Maggie went into labor. The cabin was quiet — Jim knew that if she were to cry out, she would drive the baby back and have a harder time. Jim waited all day outside and just at dusk he heard a small cry.

Blue Sky brought the baby out and handed him to Jim. He had a son! He was told to walk around the post and hold his son high so the spirits could see the baby and bless it. But Jim could only take a few steps and look at him. Then Blue Sky disappeared into the woods. Jim knew that the afterbirth must be disposed of as soon as possible by putting it high in the branches of a tree. Blue Sky was not to let anyone see her.

All these traditions were beautiful to Jim. When Blue Sky came back, Jim took the baby back into Maggie. He put the child next to her and kissed her. "Thank you, Maggie. I love you so much."

Jim looked closer at the baby and could see the cord was cut long, as was the Gros Ventre custom. It was about six inches long. They did this because they were afraid the infant would bleed to death if it were cut short. Blue Sky put some powdered root on it and put a band around the baby. She told Jim it would fall off in about four days.

Since the cord was part of the body and it must be kept close to its owner, when it fell off Blue Sky would place it in a small, fancy bag she had made and filled with sweet grass. The bag would be pinned to the baby's clothing at the back of the neck. When he started to walk, it would be tied to his waist. This bag must be taken good care of until he reached adulthood. If he should die without all his parts, his soul could not go to heaven.

Jim was amazed by this perfect creature. He looked at Maggie with a big smile. "He's beautiful. Thank you, Maggie."

"Jim," Maggie said, "we must give him two names, one Indian and one Christian, and we must have the priest baptize him."

"Maggie, we could call him 'Tchi-want,' after your father. The name 'Capture' is a good one."

"Jim, could his Christian name be Lee Roy, after my friend at Fort Benton?"

"Lee Roy it shall be."

Blue Sky came in and told Jim he must leave now. Maggie was to rest because if she were to sweat, it would hurt her milk.

Jim laughed, gave Maggie a kiss on the forehead, and left.

He stood out in front of the trading post and looked up and down the Judith River. With a big, loud yell he cried, "I have a son!"

He could hear his men all laughing and yelling back, "Congratulations, Jim!"

Jim was not allowed into the cabin for a few days. Blue Sky was there to see to that.

Blue Sky also made a belt of rawhide for Maggie about a foot wide, and immediately after delivery, tied it around her waist. This was tightened each day. Jim asked Blue Sky what it was for. She smiled, turned red and said, "Put Maggie's figure back into place for you, Jim."

Blue Sky gave Maggie medicine to make her milk come. The baby was not put on the breast immediately. Blue Sky sucked out the first milk and spit it out. She did this until the milk was the proper blue color. Jim had heard that puppies could be used to draw out the first milk too.

Jim knew that all these rules must be followed, and that is why he had brought Blue Sky to Maggie.

Jim had seen many of the women who had little milk have

their children nursed by another woman. The band always helped each other with nursing and the raising of children. Children were not weaned early. He had seen children six or more run in from play to get their mother's breast.

The trading post was a busy place that summer. Maggie's strength returned fast. The river boats came and went. By the first of August, Jim felt that things were in good enough shape to take Maggie and the baby into Fort Benton for a few days.

Little Mac, meanwhile, was becoming anxious to leave the Judith and head west to start up his own sheep ranch. This was a bad word to the cowhands, and many arguments had been held at dinner. But Little Mac thought that he could make money in sheep, and he was planning to start a ranch somewhere in western Montana.

Early one morning Jim made ready a wagon as Maggie and the baby prepared for the trip to Fort Benton. If Jim pushed it they could make it by nightfall, but they would probably turn it into a day-and-a-half trip.

The baby, wide-eyed and alert all day, seemed to enjoy riding in the wagon. Lee Roy was a good baby and growing fast. He was almost three months old.

That night Jim held the baby while Maggie prepared dinner. A delicious smell bubbled from the big old black pot that had seen many an open fire. Maggie brought Jim his supper and took the baby. She had found some wild roots and berries to add to the meat stew. Jim smiled — as he had learned a long time ago, never ask what was in it; just eat and enjoy.

"Maggie, this food is great. It seems the outdoors always makes it taste extra good."

"Thank you, Jim. I still like to cook out over a fire."

When dinner was over, Maggie brought Jim a cup of coffee and some hard sweet biscuits. "Good thing we got this coffee for them biscuits, or we couldn't eat them," Jim said.

Maggie replied, "I found out how to make them from a cook on a river boat. He said they get dry and last forever."

"Pepie's biscuits last forever but don't have that good sweet flavor."

"The difference is that new stuff, baking powder, that they brought up to me. I have the recipe here; I'm going to give it to Mr. Perkins."

"Maggie, let me see the recipe."

Maggie handed Jim a folded piece of paper, on which was written:

Good Powder Biscuits

Take about 4 cups flour
3 small spoons baking powder
Add a little salt
3 big spoons fat, from pig. Best to use a
      little more if you want rich dough,
      but the biscuits won't last as long
A cup and a half of milk

Mix the dry stuff. Cut it into the fat
with a knife, then mix with your hands. Put in
the milk a little at a time. Don't handle the
dough much. Roll on a board with a smooth jar.
Make sure the board has flour on it or the stuff
will stick. Cut with a jar top or cut in
squares. Run over the tops with milk and put on a
little sugar to give them a sweet, bright top.
Melt fat in the bottom of a pan and cook over the coals
for about 15-18 minutes.

"The baking powder and the sugar are what make them different," Maggie said.

Maggie put out buffalo robes for the night and made a bed for Lee Roy next to them. Jim checked the horse team and added wood to the fire. He took off his pants and put his gun near his head. When he got under the buffalo robes he found Maggie naked, and in a moment so was he. They made love that night under the most beautiful Montana sky, full of stars.

It was hard for Jim to get up the next morning. Maggie was already up with breakfast ready and the baby fed. "Maggie, I slept so hard they could have taken the whole camp."

"Have some food, Jim. I'll pack up so we can get on the trail."

Jim gave Maggie a big kiss. "You are so great to be with."

They arrived in Fort Benton in the early afternoon. They went straight to the T.C. Power office. Mr. Power came out to greet them. "Jim, good to see you. How are things at the Judith?"

"Better than ever. We'll check in at a hotel and then we can go over business first thing tomorrow. But I wanted to let you know we're here."

"Maggie, let me see that new baby," Power said. "He's getting big. He'll be walking by winter. Jim, you get settled, and I'll see you first thing in the morning."

"Thank you — see you tomorrow."

"Maggie, you want an early dinner at Perkins' place?"

"That sounds good, Jim. Then we won't have to take the baby out again."

When Jim and Maggie walked into Perkins', he almost knocked over half his place getting over to greet them. "Jim, Maggie, you've been in my thoughts."

"You know, Perkins, this had to be our first stop."

"Molly, Molly, come out and see who's here."

Perkins' wife Molly came out from the back room. "All that noise out here, you'd think it was a fight — Jim, Maggie, land sakes — oh, let me see that baby — give you a hug later, Jim. What a beautiful baby! What's his name?"

"How do you know it's a boy, Molly?" Perkins asked.

"I know, because he's Jim's child."

"You're right, it's a boy — name's Lee Roy."

"Jim, Maggie, sit down. Molly, get coffee. How long you here for? Where are you staying?"

"Four or five days. We're staying at the hotel," Jim said.

"No you don't, you stay at our place," Molly said as she poured coffee. "Lots of room. I'd love to have a baby in the house."

"We couldn't do that, Molly," Jim said.

"Oh yes you can. Maggie, we can go shopping and spend all your money."

Mr. Perkins said, "We have some good stew. You hungry?"

"Thank you, Perkins, we are," Jim said.

"Sure kind of you to ask us to stay at your place," Jim said later. "Mighty good stew. Well, Perkins, I got that cattle from Texas. One hell of a trip, but we should have a good herd by next spring if all goes well."

"Maybe you can start selling me beef next year, Jim. You ever hear from your brother John?"

"No, but I sure miss him. Little Mac's still with me but wants to leave this fall, start a sheep ranch west of here."

"I can't see him as a sheep man."

They all sat around and talked as Molly and Perkins took care of the customers. Maggie helped wash dishes and clean up.

"That's it for tonight. Get your wagon and come over to our place. When you get to the house I'll help you put your team up."

When Jim woke in the morning, Perkins was already back at the restaurant. Maggie and Molly were in the kitchen talking, and the baby was in a big chair taking a nap.

"Morning all. Sure slept. Getting dressed and heading over to Power's. You two be all right today?"

"Jim, be happy to see you gone. After you get done, come over to the place for dinner."

Jim walked over to Power's office. He couldn't believe how many supplies were stacked on the levee.

"Morning, Mr. Power."

"Hello, Jim. Come on in. You want coffee?"

"Sure do — thanks."

"Jim, you start on how things are at the Judith."

Jim told Power about the trip to Texas and the cattle drive back, and how the Judith was becoming not only a trading post but a ranch. They had bunk houses, a cook house, and branding pens and were cutting hay for the winter. The overland tonnage to Helena was way up and they had more and more boats dropping loads off.

Jim felt the herd would be up by a third the next year and he could start selling beef in the spring. There had been lots of healthy calves this spring.

Power wanted to know about Indian trouble.

"Well, the Sioux are a little farther east, the Blackfeet are west, and the only Indians nearby are the Gros Ventres, and they're my kin."

Power laughed. "Looks like you picked a good spot at the Judith. By the way, it came to my attention that you haven't finished transferring your new assets into the trust you established for Maggie. Best to keep up to date on that."

"Thanks for thinking of it," Jim said. "Just get everything ready and I'll take care of it."

"Jim, you know sixty-nine was a good year, shipping was down in seventy and it started back up this year. Lots of supplies from Fort Benton going to Canada. This is still their big drop-off. Also supplies to the mines out west. Here, look at

the ledger; it'll give you a good idea." As Jim looked through
the ledger book, Power commented, "What I want to show you,
Jim, is that the big years seem to be over, and cattle is good, but
I feel that freight is the future. We must build up that overland
freight to Helena."

The ledger did point out what Power was saying. Of the
12,000 tons aimed at Montana sent upriver in 1867, about 8,000
reached Fort Benton while the rest came up by wagon months
later. It had been a big passenger year, at $150 a head, with an
estimated 10,000 people coming up to get their share of the
gold.

But no new gold was discovered and travel to the territory
slowed down in 1868.

Mr. Power said, "Jim, now you can compare all those ledgers
with yours."

Jim said, "The Judith is going to make money as a trading
post, as a freight-dropping point and on cattle."

"You're right, Jim. We must keep that post going. You let me
know what supplies and help you need. Meanwhile, go take
Maggie out to see the town."

"Can I take these ledgers for the night? I want to study the
different boats and tonnages."

"Certainly, Jim. It's a pleasure doing business with you."

Jim went back over to Perkins' house, but everyone was gone.
He put the ledgers down and wandered over to the restaurant.
"Perkins, you seen a slowdown the last year and a half here in
Fort Benton?"

"Sure have, Jim. My business is down by half. Not many
people going to the gold fields, fewer passengers, more home
folk, fewer people eating out. But we still make a decent
living."

"Perkins, I'm going to take a walk around the fort and see
what's new. Tell Maggie I'll see her back here."

Jim was walking along the levee when he heard a voice. "Jim! Jim Wells!"

He turned and let out a loud yell. "I'll be Goddamned!"

"That's a poor way to greet a priest."

"Father Giorda, what are you doing in Fort Benton?"

"I could ask you the same thing. I'm here to buy supplies for St. Ignatius."

"I have Maggie with me, and our new son Lee Roy."

"Jim, I must see them."

"Father, meet us at Perkins' restaurant about 6:30. I won't tell Maggie — I'll let you surprise her."

"Good, Jim, see you at 6:30."

Jim spent the afternoon walking up and down the levee. Then he headed for the restaurant to meet Maggie and the baby. He gave Maggie a big kiss. "Sure missed you," he said affectionately. "Perkins, I have a special guest coming to dinner, so can I reserve a good table?"

Maggie was excited. "Jim, who is it?"

"Not going to tell you, or it won't be a surprise."

By 6:30 Maggie was beside herself, wondering who the special guest could be. Jim sat holding the baby while Maggie helped in the restaurant.

An old, dirty miner wandered in. He had been drinking. He looked at Maggie, then at Perkins. "Don't want any dirty squaw bringing my food," he muttered.

Perkins didn't say a word, just picked up the man and threw him out onto the street. Jim could hear Perkins yelling, "Go eat with the pigs, you smell like them." When he came back inside, he was still furious. "Sorry, Maggie, but that is Fort Benton."

"Thank you, Perkins," Jim said. "I probably would've killed him. Please, Maggie, don't let that spoil the surprise."

"I won't, Jim."

When Maggie turned around, Father Giorda was standing there.

"Oh, Father! It is so good to see you."

"Maggie, you look wonderful. Let me see that baby."

The meal was full of talk and excitement. Father Giorda said, "Jim, you've undoubtedly heard about President Grant's new policy regarding the reservations. According to this policy, the Blackfoot reservation has been given over to the Methodists, and all Jesuits are excluded. Seems you Protestants have won a battle."

"Father, Maggie and I need you to baptize the baby. That gives you another Catholic Gros Ventre, which is better than a whole tribe of Blackfeet."

Everyone laughed.

"Could you baptize the baby on Sunday?" Maggie asked.

"I would be honored to, Maggie. Sunday it will be."

"Can we use your restaurant, Mr. Perkins?" Maggie asked.

Perkins laughed. "Sounds good. A Catholic baptism in a Protestant restaurant. 'We serve good food and also baptize' — would make a good sign for the front."

Father Giorda added, "If the food kills you, you are in a holy place."

Sunday was only three days away. While Jim stayed busy going over business with Power, Maggie prepared for the baptism. She bought white cloth and made a gown for the baby, and she and Molly made special foods to serve. Jim had not seen two women so excited. The Perkins' were to stand up as godparents. Father Giorda felt this was fine, since they were good Christians even if they were Protestants, and good Christians were hard to find in the Montana Territory. T.C. Power was invited, along with some of the men at the office and their wives.

Sunday morning, Maggie woke Jim. His tub was ready and

Maggie scrubbed his back. "Your clothes are all out on the bed." Jim saw that Maggie had purchased a new suit for him. "Damn, Maggie, you went crazy. What am I going to do with a suit at the Judith?"

"Jim, if necessary I'll bury you in it, so shut up and put it on."

Maggie came out in a new dress. She looked beautiful. It was the first time Jim had seen her in a hat. It was great — it had one big feather sticking out the side.

When they arrived at the restaurant, Father Giorda said, "Well, Jim, ready to make a new Catholic?"

"Yes, Father."

He had set up a table with a bowl of water, a candle, a couple of small bottles and a towel.

The Perkins' took the baby and held his head over the bowl.

"I'm putting some holy water in the water. First I will bless the baby with the holy oils."

Father Giorda made the sign of the cross on the baby's head, lips and chest. Then he put the baby's head over the bowl and took a cup of the water. As he poured it, he said, "I baptize you, Lee Roy Wells, in the name of the Father, the Son and the Holy Ghost." He lit a candle and handed it to Perkins. "Accept this light as a sign of new light and life for this baby. You are responsible to see he is raised in the sight of God."

Then the Father took the baby and held him in the air. "Behold this new Christian."

It was a good party. People came in and out to take part in the celebration, and the word must have gotten out because many brought baby presents.

Father Giorda excused himself about 5:00 p.m., giving everyone a hug. He wanted to get on his way back to his church. Jim invited him down to the Judith, and he promised to visit.

Jim and Maggie helped clean up the restaurant, then sat to have a last cup of coffee. Perkins joined them. "Jim, you've been a good friend and you always bring lots of fun to my restaurant. I'm sure going to miss you when you leave tomorrow. When are you coming back?"

"Don't know, but you can always come to the Judith."

"Molly and I are going to make that trip some day."

That night Maggie gave Jim a big hug. "Jim, you are a great man. I'm very lucky to have you. I love you very much. It was a great day, one I will never forget."

"Thank you, Maggie. We can have a party each time you have a baby."

"Jim, you go to sleep. No babies for a while."

Jim and Maggie were up early the next morning. They packed and said their goodbyes to the Perkins', then went over to pick up supplies from Power's warehouse. "Mr. Power, you know where I might pick up a milk cow and a couple of pigs?" Jim asked.

Power replied, "There's a farmer on the edge of town who raises pigs. He also has a couple of milk cows. You don't like milking them beef cows?"

"No, they're a little hard to tame. Mr. Power, I'll keep the reports coming in. But as I said, if we get through this winter, things will be as stable as we could hope for."

"Jim, have a good trip."

"Thanks, we will."

Jim climbed up in the wagon, which was loaded not only with supplies from Power's warehouse but with all the things Maggie had purchased in town.

"Maggie, I want to make a stop and try to buy a couple of pigs and a milk cow. We're going to need milk for the baby."

"Jim, those chickens I got off the boat are laying pretty well. I'd like to have a good milk cow too."

"If we get one, it'll keep Pepie busy taking care of it. You think Pepie is going to marry Blue Sky?"

"You know, I'm teaching Blue Sky English and Pepie Gros Ventre, so you might be right."

They weren't very far out of Fort Benton when Jim spotted the farm down by the river. Jim drove right up to the house. A man came out. "Hi, my name's Jim Wells; I come from the Judith. My partner's Mr. Power." Jim got off the wagon to shake the man's hand.

"My name is Jon." The man had a funny way of talking.

"You're not from these parts?" Jim asked.

"I came upriver two years ago, from Sweden."

Jim told Jon that he would like three pigs, one sow and two boars, one to kill and cure for meat, the other to breed the sow.

Jon said, "The cow will be seventy-five dollars, plus twenty-five each for the pigs."

"That's lots of money for a milk cow and pigs," Jim said.

"Yes, it is, Mr. Wells, but it cost me a lot to get them up here on the boat, and they are just starting to pay for themselves."

Jim wasn't going to argue. He knew how hard it was to get stock up to the Territory, and his milk cow and pigs looked good. "I'll take them. I need some rope for the cow. I'll need to re-stack my supplies and put the pigs in the back of the wagon."

Jon had a ramp that was wagon-high, and he drove the pigs right up the ramp. "The sow's about due to have a litter soon. The big pig's the best one to save for breeding — too tough to eat."

Jim got a receipt for the cow and pigs when he paid Jon. "Thank you, Jon. If you get to the Judith area, come visit."

"Thank you for your business. The cow will lead easy — she's a good cow. Remember, you must milk her every morning and evening or she'll dry up on you. You can give the milk to the pigs. Here is an extra pail — you may need it."

"Thank you again," Jim said as he took the pail. He looked at Maggie and started to laugh. "I haven't milked a cow since I was a boy."

"Jim, I've never milked a cow," said Maggie.

They set up camp that night along the Missouri River. Jim milked the cow and staked her out with the team. "Those damned pigs stink. We'll have to burn the wagon when we get to the Judith. Good thing the wind blows through."

"Jim, I don't know a thing about pigs. The only pigs I have had are those salt meats you get from the boats."

"I hope Pepie knows how to smoke a pig."

When they arrived back at the Judith, no one could believe Jim had three big pigs in the back of his wagon.

"Pepie, you unload. I'll get some of the boys to make a pen for the pigs and put the cow in the branding pen for now. Pepie, I hope you can milk?"

"I can, Boss. I'd like to have milk for cooking."

The pig had a litter of twelve the week after they returned from Fort Benton. Pepie made a smokehouse and killed and prepared the smaller boar. Pepie loved the cow, and Jim and Maggie could hear him out by the pen, talking to her. He named her Maria, after his mother.

One day Pepie came to Jim and asked for a few days off. He wanted to take Blue Sky off and find a priest so they could get married.

"Congratulations, Pepie," Jim said. "Glad you came to Montana?"

"Yes. Montana's cold, but now I'm not," Pepie laughed.

Jim and Maggie had a party for Blue Sky and Pepie the night before they left to find a priest. Jim gave them a wagon and team to use, and Maggie prepared food and bedding for them.

"They sure look happy, even though they can't understand each other," Jim said.

Maggie laughed. "I think they understand each other very well."

Pepie and Blue Sky returned ten days later. Blue Sky packed her things from Maggie's and Jim's cabin and moved over to Pepie's.

"They look so happy," Maggie said.

"Maybe they'll stay now," Jim said. "Pepie seems happy here. I'll build them a bigger cabin next summer."

The first light snow came in mid-September.

"I hope we have a mild winter. It'll help the herd get settled in," Jim said to Maggie.

"If you follow the animals, it should be a mild winter. The squirrels and groundhogs aren't working very hard."

It had been a quiet summer for the Judith regarding the Indians. President Grant was under pressure because of Sand Creek in 1864 and the Fetterman Massacre of 1866, in which Captain William Fetterman and eighty men were tricked and slaughtered by Sioux. He had appointed a few Quakers and a number of Army Officers to advisory posts on the plains. On the other hand, in 1870 a Major Baker charged into a Piegan village on the Marias River and killed 173 members of the tribe, including many women and children. This caused Congress to once and for all remove the Indian Bureau from the War Department.

But Jim felt that the Indians were still being pushed, and it was only a matter of time before they reacted. There was talk about a reservation for the Gros Ventres up around the town of Harlem, which was northeast of the Judith.

Back at the post the cattle were moved down from the hill and put along the Judith River for winter protection, not only from the cold weather but from wolves and other wild animals. The haystacks were not to be opened to the cattle until the snow was too deep for them to dig for dry grass. Jim felt he was ready for a long winter and could bring his herd through.

The weather grew cold, but the first big snow didn't come until the first of December. That storm left about four feet of snow, but it was followed by warm weather and the snow melted. But by Christmas about ten feet of snow was on the ground.

The men would go out to check the herd and only stay out a couple of hours, returning to the buildings to warm up.

Jim told the men that they could make extra money by shooting and skinning wolves. It gave them something else to do. By the end of December, over one hundred wolf pelts were curing in the barn.

At Christmas Jim and Maggie threw a party for everyone at the trading post. Jim cut a large fir, which Maggie and Blue Sky decorated with popcorn and ribbons. And Jim broke out the barrel of good whiskey he had kept. Some of the men played fiddles and flutes and everyone ate and danced.

Jim gave Maggie a pearl necklace. He bought new clothes and sheepskin jackets for all the men. He gave Blue Sky a bolt of material, and made the baby a rocking horse with a mane and tail. Pepie made a little saddle and each of the men added decorations to the horse.

Pepie gave Maggie a nativity group. It was hand-carved of wood and painted. Maggie said, "Oh, Pepie, it is beautiful. It will always have a place of honor in our house."

After the party, Jim and Maggie went back to their cabin where she gave him his present. She had made him a pair of new leather pants and a shirt, covered with beadwork.

"Maggie, I'll be the best-dressed man on the Judith. Thank you for a good Christmas."

January and February became extremely cold. Jim went out to check on the cattle himself.

"Jim, how do the cattle look?" Maggie asked.

"I tell you, Maggie, I can't figure it out. It's so damn cold but they're still moving. I hope the weather starts to break soon."

"Jim, believe me. It was a late winter so we will have an early spring."

"Keep those good thoughts, Maggie."

Maggie and Blue Sky spent many days talking and sewing and watching Lee Roy. Jim spent a lot of time fixing up the inside of the trading post, where the men gathered together to play cards. The big wood stove made it the warmest place at the Judith.

By mid-March the weather started to break, and Jim felt the worst had passed. He had been told over and over never to trust the weather in Montana, and he could remember the winter he and his brother John had spent out in the open and how it had almost cost them their lives. God, how cold it had been with that wind blowing and no way to get warm.

"Jim, I think Blue Sky is going to have a baby," Maggie said one evening.

"Boy, old Pepie's going to be a happy man."

"You know, Lee Roy was baptized but I still want him to go through the tribal name-giving ceremony."

"Explain that one to me, Maggie."

"It will take place when our boy is about three years old. The name, for the Gros Ventres, will signify the spirit living in the child and will be his gift to the tribal community, both his white and his Indian community. I would like to ask my father to bestow the name."

"Maggie, why wait three years?"

"The mysterious spirit rains down his seed during springtime on Mother Earth. From Mother Earth comes all beauty and life. So every creature has some power, some spirit within it. We come from Mother Earth. It is important that this power or spirit within us be identified and revered.

"It takes time to perceive the power, the ability to identify it. Only when the child has lived three years would my father be able to identify the spirit within him. It is a very spiritual ceremony.

"Jim, when I became a Catholic the priest told me that the naming ceremony was an outward sign of inner grace for my people. As with baptism, the naming sets the child apart for a spiritual destiny. The name is more than a label to distinguish him; it is his destiny. As he grows he will be honored in his life for his great deeds, which our baby will, and people will say, 'He was being true to the spirit within him.' So with your baptism and mine, our baby will have Indian ways and as a Christian child, will learn the implications gradually, as he grows and begins to know his ways and his faith."

"Maggie, you put things great. You know I want our children to know both ways. At least the Jesuits want your ways to exist and see their true meaning. Maggie, I forgot what brought this up."

"I told you I think Blue Sky is with child."

"That's right. But Maggie, anything you want for our baby is fine with me."

"Thank you, Jim, for your trust and support." Maggie gave Jim a big hug.

It was only a couple of weeks later that Pepie came over to Jim with a big smile. "Boss, Blue Sky's going to have a baby. I'm so happy."

"Pepie, I'm happy for you. Come, let's have a whiskey on that good news." And Jim felt that Pepie would make a good father. He was very proud of his wife, Blue Sky.

"Pepie, you'll have to change your name to Padre."

"No, Boss, if I was a padre, I couldn't make babies, only bless them."

They had a couple of drinks, then Pepie had to get back to his chores. Jim really liked Pepie and was glad he had come up north with him. Jim also felt lucky that he had been able to keep Little Mac through the winter, but knew that Mac would be leaving. He would miss him.

Jim felt better and better about the Judith. It would be great to start seeing families here. He could set aside land for some shops and maybe a small hotel. Now that he thought about it, he could see a hotel at the Judith with a restaurant, run by Perkins. He laughed to himself.

It was an early spring. The snow melted quickly, and a watch was set up on the Missouri for the ice flow to make sure they didn't get flooded.

Little Mac came in to tell Jim that he was leaving. "Jim, you've been a good friend. If I can't make it, can I come back?"

"Mac, you're always welcome and will always be a partner with me. But knowing you, you'll do good."

They gave each other a handshake and a hug.

"Maggie, you and the baby take good care. I'll miss that baby."

Jim stood with his arm around Maggie as they watched Mac ride off. "Damn, I miss him already, and he ain't even out of sight," Jim said.

"He is a good, honest friend, Jim."

In early June, the Judith was visited by a Jesuit named Father Jerome D'Aste, a gentle and very loveable Italian from Genoa. He was welcomed by all and given a guest room.

"Father, what brings you down to the Judith?" Jim asked.

"Father Giorda left St. Mary's for St. Ignatius so I was given this area, and I thought the best way to see it would be to get on my horse and travel."

"Father, are you by yourself? You'll get yourself killed or lost."

"Garibaldi drove me from my homeland; I can survive a few Indians in Montana. I'm looking for the Gros Ventre camps and the Assiniboines. Maggie, has your baby been baptized?"

"Yes, Father, by Giorda."

"Oh, now I know who you are. Father Giorda spoke so well of you."

"He is a good man," Jim said. "Father, this is Pepie and his wife Blue Sky."

They exchanged greetings and sat.

"Father, please give our food a blessing. It usually needs it if Pepie cooked it."

"Jim!" Maggie scolded.

"Bless this food and the hands that fixed it. Amen. Jim, have you ever heard the story of how Father Giorda was almost killed at St. Mary's?" Father D'Aste went on.

"I sure did, but tell it for Pepie."

"If you know Father Giorda, he is a good man and spends much of his time making the rounds of Indian tribes and missions. But one night a drunken Indian took a shot at him as he sat at his desk!"

"And, Pepie, this padre is riding all over this country alone," Jim said.

"No, Jim, he has God with him. He'll be all right."

"Thank you, Pepie," Father D'Aste said.

The Father said Mass for the people at the trading post early the next morning. After Mass, Maggie and Blue Sky made him a big breakfast and Pepie packed him some supplies.

"Father, you always have a bunk and food here. You're always welcome," Jim told him.

"Thank you, Jim. God bless you all."

"Them Jesuits are crazy, the way they wander around this country," Jim remarked.

"That's true, Jim, but they've been out here a lot longer than you and most whites, and not many have been killed. Maybe because they won't carry a weapon and are willing to learn to speak and live the Indian way."

"You're right, Maggie. The Jesuits do look after the Indians and don't take their traditions away."

On June 20, 1872, Lee Roy had his first birthday. He was becoming a handful and Maggie needed to keep an eye on him all the time.

"Jim, could you build a fence around an area behind the trading post, so I can put Lee Roy outside and not worry about that river?"

Jim fixed up an area and put some logs and sand from the river in it for Lee Roy to play in. "Got to get that kid a brother or sister to play with, Maggie."

"No, not yet. He will have Pepie's baby to play with."

"You're right. We should wait, but not too long."

Things fell into a routine at the post. Boats arrived, supplies were loaded into a wagon for Helena, calves were brought down to be branded. Bulls that were castrated, cows that didn't have calves, and older bulls were put in a pen to be sold to the Army or at Fort Benton.

The leftover testicles were cooked by Pepie. "They're good when they're young," he said. Castration was done by a sharp knife, and a handful of salt was rubbed into the wound.

Jim sent a monthly report off to T.C. Power in Fort Benton. But he didn't make the trip often himself — he was happier staying around the Judith.

In July, Maggie, Blue Sky and Lee Roy went over to visit the Gros Ventre summer camp. Maggie returned, saddened. Her band was becoming very poor and there weren't many buffalo. The Army was trying to put them on a reservation, telling them if they did they would be fed and cared for like the other Indians on reservations.

"Maggie, can I send them some beef?"

"Jim, it isn't beef. It is very hard to see my proud people, who always helped the whites, now becoming beggars. It is not right."

"Maggie, what can I do?"

"As things become harder, please don't turn away from these people. I want our children to know them. As they get older I want them to spend more time with my band."

"Maggie, I promise, as long as I'm alive our kids will always be a part of your people. As you know, your family saved my life and I'm part of you and them." Jim felt lost — what could he do? He hated to see Maggie hurt, and she was hurt.

Jim knew that Indians had helped many whites travel across the territory, providing food, drink, shelter and guides. The Indians, unless provoked, were fascinated by the whites and all their contraptions, and could not imagine that there would not be room enough for everyone. Nor could they imagine the kind of hate they would inspire in the growing number of white settlers.

Maggie's people were hunters. They supplemented their food supply with some fish and wild vegetables, but their staple was the wonderful buffalo. Jim remember his first time in a camp among all the brightly painted new buffalo-hide tents. The hunting tipi was small, but the camp or ceremonial tipi stood twenty feet high and measured thirty feet across inside. It required up to fifty buffalo to make.

Jim had loved to watch and help as the tipis were put up. First the main poles were raised and lashed together; then the smaller poles were set in place, and the buffalo skins were pulled up and laced together with sinew. Then the tipi pegs were driven into the ground to hold the lower edge firm. The tipi was perfect for the needs of the Indian. It was easily moved, and when arranged on horseback could serve as a platform for carrying goods. In winter, a lining kept out the cold air; in the summer the skins could be rolled up to admit a breeze. The fire was always directly in the center, so that the smoke went directly out the hole on top.

Jim would hate to see all this life disappear. He must ask Maggie where the tipi was that had been given to them when they were married. Jim wanted to keep it and set it up someday for his children to see.

Jim's thoughts kept going back to what he had learned from the Indians. Before the whites ruined things, the Indian furs were of the highest quality. The hides could be treated to make them tough enough to use as war shields, or cured to make the softest leather. The coat of almost any animal could be utilized by the Indian. First the skin was scraped and tanned with a mixture that might include liver and brains, and then it was thoroughly soaked in water. Jim watched this process over and over in amazement, because he had helped his father tan leather, but it had never been as fine as what the Indians made. They would wring out the skin and stretch it over a frame to dry. When dry, it was ready for cutting and sewing into clothes, bags, pouches, footwear, arrow cases, or many thousands of other items used in the daily life of the Indian.

The Gros Ventres were the best he had ever seen at preparing the skins.

Furthermore, anything the Indian made of leather he always decorated. Clothes would be fringed, embroidered, painted, or covered with beadwork, shells, quill work, or feathers.

The Gros Ventres were also good weavers. Jim had seen shirts, dresses, belts, sashes, chief's blankets, shoulder blankets, ponchos, and other items made by the Indian weavers.

Jim walked back into the cabin. He gave Maggie a big hug. "Maggie, I'm sorry your people are suffering, but I really feel it will get a lot worse, and no way can it be stopped."

"I know, Jim. "

The trading post and ranch were making a good profit.

Jim raised the wages of all his men. "You men are making me money. If I share with you, you'll stay and help me make more money. I have one good bunch here at the Judith. It makes me want to stay longer."

Each of the men came up, thanked Jim and shook his hand.

In early September they had some early cold rains at the Judith, and Jim's cough came back again. He was having trouble breathing.

"Maggie, I'm going to Fort Benton to see a doctor."

"No, Jim, I'll take you to see our medicine man. Tomorrow."

Blue Sky was to take care of Lee Roy, and Maggie made provisions for the trip. Jim was feeling so bad he couldn't protest.

"Maggie, have Cap cut out a couple of good beef cattle to take to the camp for a feast."

"That will be good, Jim. I'll ask him."

Jim and Maggie went on horseback because it was faster, even if they were slowed by those stubborn steers. They camped by the Missouri River. Jim was up most of the night with his cough and fever.

"I hope I don't get as sick as the last time you had to take care of me."

"Jim, you'll be fine as soon as the medicine man sees you."

"I hope so."

They arrived at the camp late the next day. Even as sick as Jim was, he could see how the band's life had deteriorated. The whole camp came out to greet Jim and Maggie. Capture walked up to them.

"He is very sick and must see the medicine man," Maggie started in. "Can we take him to the medicine lodge?"

The medicine man came out of his lodge. He was now very old. He walked up to Jim, touched his head and pointed to his lodge. Jim was taken into the lodge and placed on a bed of buffalo robes. He heard the medicine man telling everyone to leave. Then Jim saw the sacred fire in the middle and remembered that this medicine man dedicated his fire to thunder; his power came from the eagle.

Jim was given something to drink and almost instantly felt the heat rise in his body. He heard the medicine man start to sing and the beating of drums in the distance. His head started to spin and he felt that he was leaving his body, from his toes, progressing to his knees, chest, arms and head. Now Jim was standing, looking down at his own body. He could see the medicine man singing and rubbing medicine on him. He knew he must not leave this lodge or he would not find his body again.

It was only moments before he could feel his body calling him back. He opened his eyes and felt cool water on his head.

"How do you feel, Jim?" the medicine man asked.

"Very weak."

"I'll call Maggie — she will make food for you."

The medicine man put his head out of the lodge and in a few moments, Maggie was at the lodge with broth made from herbs and marrow from buffalo bones.

"Jim, you must eat this."

"Maggie, it's morning already? I thought I was only asleep a few minutes."

"No, Jim, you have been asleep for three days. But you are well now — please drink this. You must eat."

Three days! It was hard to believe. But his fever and cough were gone.

They stayed another couple of days until Jim felt strong again.

"Thank you again, Capture, for everything. Please see that the medicine man gets a little extra beef."

"He will not eat beef; in fact he eats very little of anything. He says the grandfathers feed his body."

"He is a powerful man."

"Yes, Jim. He has many powers, but he is our last. No one in our band has a calling to be a medicine man."

When Jim and Maggie were back on the trail, Jim asked Maggie, "How does someone know he's supposed to be a medicine man?"

"Jim, every Indian man must go off alone and fast and pray in the wilderness in order to communicate personally with his guardian spirit, who will tell him his role in the band."

"Maggie, you think everyone will be told?"

"Yes, Jim."

"Then why will there be no new medicine man?"

"My father feels it is a very bad omen on our tribe. But we are safe as long as this medicine man lives."

"But Maggie, he is so old."

"Old, but very powerful."

"Maggie, you know, I felt I left my body at the medicine lodge."

"Yes, Jim, you leave it so it can rest and be made healthy."

"I swear I saw the medicine man rub my body with herbs. Then he blew smoke all over me."

"You were sick from a demon. When he blows smoke into your ears, nostrils and mouth, it drives out the demons within."

"Our doctors could learn a lot from your people."

Back at the trading post, everyone continued to prepare for the winter. The snows were deep by mid-November and it was hard to get from the cabin to the trading post, where the men would gather during the day to keep warm and play cards.

On November 26, 1872, a son was born to Blue Sky and Pepie. Pepie broke into the trading post. "I have a son, helped into the world by Maggie. A son!"

"Hey, Pepie, what're you going to name him?" Cap asked.

"His name will be Jesus Roxas."

"That's one big name for a little boy," the Kid said.

"He's not going to be small for long. He's going to be a big man."

Everyone laughed. Jim broke out a box of cigars he had hidden, along with a jug of whiskey. "Come on, men, it's time to celebrate. The Judith has just grown by one."

Christmas came and a party was held for all at the Judith. Then they all settled in for the next two and a half months of tough winter weather. Jim caught up on some old newspapers and the campaign against the Indians in the Southwest.

Walter S. Schuyler was a name Jim saw a lot of. Schuyler had graduated from West Point in 1870, and had joined the Fifth Cavalry in Arizona to round up all the "hostiles" and put them on reservations. This was considered to be one tough assignment. The desert was inhospitable, and the Apaches were known as the most clever and treacherous of the native tribes. Still, Schuyler managed well in Arizona. He organized his troops efficiently and was unrelenting, finally driving group after group to defeat. Jim could imagine Schuyler coming north as soon as things were settled down in Arizona. The Army was pushing west from the Dakota, north from Arizona, and east from Washington. All Indians would be defeated and contained.

More news came to the Judith about the Indian wars. General George Armstrong Custer was working hard to control and annihilate the Indians. Back in 1867 he had been court-martialled for desertion, among other things, though he himself had ordered twelve soldiers shot for the same offense. After sitting home and brooding for a year, Custer had been ordered to take up against the Comanches and Kiowas in the Wichita Mountains. Descending on those tribes, Custer had declared that any warrior not killed during battle would be hung, that all women and children would be made war prisoners, all horses slaughtered and all tipis torched.

Jim followed each story and as ever, hoped that all the fighting would stay out of the Montana Territory.

"What do you think about this General Custer?" Jim said to Cap. "He seems to think he's above the rules, and he's an Indian hater too. I don't trust him."

The summer of 1873 saw a good year for the Judith. The settlement now had a small hotel and a couple of businesses. The ranch was also growing and it was a bigger job each spring, with calving, branding and culling the cattle. The stock was looking better each year. Jim was becoming a rich man, but he always shared his money with his men. Maggie would say, "Jim, you know I've no use for that money. I can still trade for what I want."

In the fall, Maggie became pregnant with their second child. Jim was very happy. "At least you beat Pepie and Blue Sky on their second."

"You've talked to Pepie and Blue Sky lately?"

It was true — there would be two new babies at the Judith in the spring.

Jim always felt like a big bear going into hibernation in the fall. So much time was spent preparing for winter, drying and salting meat, cutting hay, moving cattle into sheltered areas, cutting wood and preparing all the buildings.

Jim would make a couple of trips that winter to Fort Benton to work with Power and prepare for the next summer. Power was very pleased with the partnership and the profit the Judith was making. He told Jim, "If only some of my other ventures would work out as well."

Power was putting his own boats into operation and his warehouses were the biggest in Fort Benton. But the Judith still made profit on early and late boats and direct freight to Helena and posts around the Judith.

Meanwhile, Fort Benton had become the supply center for southern Alberta. In 1870, the powerful Hudson Bay Company had sent a train of bull teams loaded with furs to Fort Benton for shipment east. Bismarck, then in Dakota Territory and called Edwinton, was founded in 1872 when the Northern Pacific reached that point. Fort Benton enabled it to develop. The Bismarck-Fort Benton river route was also a trade route of great importance to Montana and southern Canada.

Jim was amused to follow the great steamboat race that year. The Far West and the Nellie Peck raced from Sioux City to Fort Benton, the Far West beating the Nellie Peck into the Fort Benton levee by an hour or so. Both boats unloaded and turned around, the Nellie Peck six hours behind. Then the Peck passed the Far West at Fort Berthold, but ran aground a few hundred miles downriver. The Far West sailed past, getting to Sioux City three hours ahead and setting a round-trip record from Sioux City to Benton and back of seventeen days, twenty hours, never surpassed. The distance was 2,800 miles.

In the spring of 1874, another son was born to Jim and Maggie. They named him William. Within two weeks Blue Sky gave birth to a son, named James Roxas, after Jim.

"We need to get that priest down here again, so he can baptize the new members of the Judith," Jim said.

Jim continued to feel the white invasion coming closer and closer to the Montana Territory. Because of Custer's expedition into the Black Hills in 1874, whites were pouring into the heart of the new Sioux-Cheyenne homeland looking for gold. Though the Indian Bureau and Army were supposed to protect the Indians against trespassing, it seemed obvious to Jim that no one would do anything about it. Soon the Indians began attacking the gold diggers, who then had an excuse to attack the Indians.

In the summer of 1874, Fort Benton merchants could see signs of an approaching boom. Jim and Power were uneasy. If the Judith and Fort Benton merchants saw a boom approaching, so did others. Carroll's was founded near the mouth of the Musselshell by men connected with the gigantic Diamond R Transportation company, which had 1,200 oxen and four hundred mules, hundreds of horses and many men employed. The Judith was still a good drop-off point and cattle was becoming the main business, but Jim didn't want to lose the shipping trade.

In early fall, Father Giorda arrived at the Judith on his rounds of the Indian tribes. This was a great day and Maggie and Blue Sky made preparations for the baptism of their new babies.

Jim and Pepie took Father Giorda over to the trading post for a little whiskey from the new batch that had come upriver. "Father, it's always a pleasure when you come to visit. How long can you stay?" Jim asked.

"Only a day. I have a lot of work," Father Giorda replied. "As you know, Jim, the government has a hard time keeping its promises. But finally, twenty years none too soon at St. Ignatius

Mission, the government will come through. We will get twenty-one hundred dollars for this year, and the same for the next two years, for the lodging, food and instruction for approximately forty Indian children."

"Father, I hope you get a mission out in our area. In the next couple of years we'll need one for our kids. We're going to need a school," Jim said.

"Jim, the Jesuits and Sisters are spread thin in Montana Territory. It's hard to keep up with what we have now."

The evening conversation went on until early morning on the changes in the Montana Territory.

The next morning a Mass was held and both babies were baptized. Jim and Maggie were godparents for Pepie and Blue Sky's baby, and Pepie and Blue Sky were godparents for Jim and Maggie's baby.

A large feast was held after Mass.

In mid-afternoon, Father Giorda gave his blessing and said goodbye to his friends. He had a long journey if he was to visit all the tribes in the area. Maggie was always sad to see Father Giorda leave.

The battles for the land went on and Jim followed the government's feeble attempts at protection. By mid-1875, there were nearly 25,000 whites on Indian land in the Dakotas. Jim could see that the government was trying everything to start a fight with the Sioux, and was certain that Indian wars would soon be in Montana. When word came of Custer's defeat at the Little Big Horn, in June of 1876, no one at the post mourned.

"From what I hear, Custer was crazy," Jim said. "Had to have his men singing special songs marching in to shoot up villages, women and children massacred too. A sick and crazy man."

"Why does the government allow sick and crazy men to be in charge?" Maggie asked.

"Because they get the job done," Jim replied.

Meanwhile Chief Joseph of the Nez Perce was fleeing six companies of infantry, five troops of cavalry, a hundred Indian scouts, two field guns, and many wagons. Word was sent out to all the towns in the area; the Judith received a message asking for volunteers as scouts or civilian military. Jim talked to his men and said, "Any that want to can volunteer. But I'm going to make sure, if I can, that the Indians get fair treatment."

By the time Jim arrived, Chief Joseph was trapped up in the Bear's Paw Mountains of Montana. It was only a matter of days for him. Most of the people in both camps stayed out of the battles, only wanting to survive. A stray bullet hit Chief Looking Glass in the head and he died. With Joseph for four months, he had helped lead this small army of Indians more than thirteen hundred miles, and they had always defeated the United States Army until this moment.

So at last Joseph ordered a flag of truce be raised over his makeshift village. There remained with him eighty-seven warriors, forty of them wounded, one hundred eighty women and one hundred forty-seven children, many of them ill and with open wounds.

When Joseph surrendered, he said:

"I am tired of fighting. My people ask me for food and I have none to give. It is cold and we have no blankets, no wood. My people are starving to death. Where is my little daughter? I do not know. Perhaps even now she is freezing to death. Hear me, my chiefs! I have fought. But from where the sun now stands, Joseph will fight no more forever."

Even the Generals to whom Chief Joseph surrendered respected him. Jim was in the camp of volunteers at the base of the mountains when he heard the news of the surrender. "We must always remember this day," he said to himself. "October 4, 1877. The last day of freedom for the Indians." And Jim found himself in tears when Chief Joseph, holding his head high, rode surrounded by guards through the camp and received a huge cheer from the volunteers, followed by cheers from the Army troops.

On his way home to the Judith, Jim stopped in at Little Mac's sheep ranch in the Smith River Valley. Little Mac had gone into business with the Smith brothers, John and Bill. Sheep matured more quickly than cattle, and one could get cash on hand as soon as they were sheared, but sheep destroyed the cattle grazing land. Not much good feeling existed between the sheepmen and the cattlemen.

Jim was greeted with open arms by his friend Little Mac. "Jim, did you have any trouble finding me?"

"No problem, Mac. I just followed the sheep smell from ten to fifteen miles out."

"Jim, get the bottle off the shelf. We have to have a drink to celebrate your being here at Smith Valley. What brings you this way?"

"I was called by the Army as a volunteer to fight the Nez Perce. Truth is, I didn't go to fight. And I got there too late anyway."

"Yes, Jim, they went right through here but didn't get my sheep. But they killed a friend of mine, Murphy. You remember Father Murphy?"

Jim did remember him. He was wanted for a murder he had committed in self-defense. He had come out west to raise sheep and had worked for Mac and the Smith brothers.

"Mac," Jim started in, "are you happy raising sheep?"

"I'm making good money but I'd like to sell out and go back to the east coast for a while."

Mac had started out with nine hundred prime mixed Cotswold and Merino ewes from Idaho. He had driven them all the way to Montana. The first winter they bred their nine hundred ewes with only Merino rams. Within two years they were shearing fifteen thousand pounds of wool, which sold at thirty-five cents a pound. The flocks thrived on the grass in the Judith Basin.

"Jim, how are you doing at the Judith?"

Jim told Mac that the river freight was up and down and that it was still a fight to establish a port below Fort Benton for the early and late boats. The things that were making money for Jim were the ranch and the cattle. His biggest customer was still the Army, and his beef was their choice.

Jim knew that Mac had the same problems as he did — rattlesnakes, blizzards, drought, straying bands of hostile Indians, and poisonous weeds which, in this area, included the roots of wild parsley, black fern, and anise. Hungry animals ate their fill. But with all the problems, the cattle and sheep thrived.

Jim told Mac he had two boys, with another child due the next spring. "How many kids are you going to have, Jim?" Mac asked.

"Maggie wants a big family." Jim started to cough.

"You still got that bad cough? It's going to kill you someday."

"I know it."

Jim stayed the night with Mac and was off early the next morning for home. "Mac, please come and see us at the Judith."

"I will, Jim."

The spring of 1877 saw the arrival of river boats early, with the good flow of the Missouri and an early ice break-up. With the mild winter, the cattle had an easy time and the loss of calves was low. It looked like a good year for Jim and the Judith. As more and more Army troops were stationed in Montana, Jim could move all excess cattle early in the spring, which was also good for Jim. The Army would come to the Judith and move their own cattle.

Jim made many trips to Fort Benton that summer, working closely with Mr. Power. Fort Benton was becoming a big city. It must have had a population of five hundred people. But the thing that interested Jim was that there were now four firms dealing with freight: T.C. Power and Bro., I.G. Baker and Co., Murphy Neel and Co., and Kleinschmidt and Bro.. The town had two druggists, doctors, a tinsmith, two saddlers, stables, blacksmiths, a boot maker, a ferry and a newspaper. The big talk was that they were to build a Catholic church, which would be the town's first place of worship.

On one of his trips to Fort Benton, Jim made an appointment with a doctor to check on his cough. The doctor gave him some medicine and told him, "There isn't much you can do — it's one of those coughs that will stay with you all your life."

Jim and Maggie's third child was born on September 12, 1878. She was their first daughter, named Mary Wells. With the arrival, Jim knew he would have to stay around the Judith that winter.

Jim received word that Father Camillus Imoda had been sent to Fort Benton to build the first Catholic church. It made Maggie happy. She could go to Fort Benton with Jim to attend Mass, and they could also have Mary baptized if a Jesuit didn't come to the Judith.

Jim was also given the task of finding a school teacher for his children and the other children at the Judith. Maggie had been working with her children and Pepie's children, but it was time for a real teacher. Jim put the word out in Fort Benton to find a teacher off one of the early boats in the spring.

Maggie didn't want to wait until spring to have Mary baptized, so near the end of October, Jim and Maggie took Mary into Fort Benton to have Father Camillus Imoda baptize her. Again the Perkins' were asked to be godparents. A party was held at their restaurant. Father Imoda was a very pleasant priest. He was pleased to do the baptism. He was in the process of building the frame church, and told Jim and Maggie that if they waited until spring, Mary could be baptized in a church. But Maggie always felt winter was a dangerous time for children, and she didn't want to wait.

While in Fort Benton Jim learned that Little Mac was satisfying his hankering to go back to the States. Bill and John Smith had bought out his share, though if he wanted he could come back and ranch on his own. But everyone was talking about how he had broken the law of the West — he padlocked the door of his shack.

Little Mac told everyone, "It might be, that on my return, someone would step across the threshold with me. Her sensitivities should not be offended by the sights and smells that would accumulate if the cabin were left open to anyone who chose to enter during my absence."

So when the shearing was over, he left his own sheep in the care of herders and caught the last boat of the summer from Fort Benton. Jim had just missed him, but he knew that Little Mac would be back.

All the papers around Montana were carrying a story about John Wesley Powell, the director of the United States Geological Survey. He had written a report proposing certain legislation to prevent the inevitable ruin of the northern Plains resulting from the thoughtless ravaging of the white man. He stated that Americans must preserve the best of Indian civilization. Powell analyzed grasses and learned what made the western grasses so nutritious, so hardy against the elements, and yet so easily destroyed by the white man's presence.

Everyone thought he was crazy and that Montana Territory

could handle anything man wanted to do to it, but Jim thought he sounded like a smart man.

Things were changing. Gold was discovered in the Bear's Paw Mountains in the Judith Basin in 1879, which put a rush on supplies from the Judith and Fort Benton. And twenty-five thousand bushels of grain were grown and threshed around Fort Benton that year. But freighters and stage men were still having their usual troubles with hostile Sioux.

The Judith built a small schoolhouse and Jim was able to find a teacher, a woman from New York named Alicia Stockwell. With the finding of gold and the increase of trade, the Judith had a town of almost a hundred souls now; the school had a dozen students. The school and its students were Maggie's responsibility.

The winter of 1880 was also a mild one. It was good for the cattle that losses would be low, but to Montanans it meant a slow start for the boats, low water, May and June arrivals only after rains and run-off.

With the mines and the Army, Jim and his men continued to prosper.

In August of 1880, a second daughter was born to Jim and Maggie. Now they had four children: Lee, William, Mary and Emma.

The Wells family planned a trip to Fort Benton for the first week in September to have Emma baptized. Once again it was a shock for both Jim and Maggie to see the amount of growth in the town. The old Overland Hotel had been remodeled, the Twig House was enlarged and was now the Chotral house, and there were two banks, the Bank of Northern Montana and First National Bank. W.H. Buck had built a three-story brick building, T.C. Power and Brothers had built a two-story brick building. The Catholic church was complete, which meant that

Emma could be baptized there. The total tonnage was 12,460 upriver and 2,250 downriver, in addition to 1800 passengers.

Fort Benton was a thriving center.

On this trip, Jim and Maggie took Pepie and Blue Sky to be the godparents of Emma. Jim booked a room at the Overland Hotel, but he almost had to fight to take it. The hotel was owned by a John Hunsberger, who didn't like Mexicans or Indians.

Jim told Hunsberger, "If I'm not going to stay here you won't have a hotel for anyone to stay in, so give me two rooms or I destroy this place."

Hunsberger told the clerk, "Give Mr. Wells the room he wants." He turned to Jim. "How long are you staying, Mr. Wells?"

"Only as long as I must."

They were shown to their rooms. Jim said, "Pepie and Blue Sky, get cleaned up. I'll take you to dinner at Perkins' restaurant. He can cook a hell of a lot better than you, Pepie."

"Better see this great cooking," Pepie said.

The rooms were much nicer than Jim remembered. They unpacked and Jim said, "Put your best on, Maggie. We'll surprise the Perkins'."

Pepie and Blue Sky were in the lobby waiting for Jim and Maggie. There were a lot of people in the lobby and the four of them received a few stares. "I guess we look strange to the newcomers," Jim said.

Pepie smiled. "Just think, Boss — a white man, a Mexican and two Indian women, with you and me in buckskin."

They went down the block to Perkins' restaurant. As Jim walked in, Perkins let out a yell. "Jim, I heard you were in town! It took you a long time to get to my place." The two men gave each other a hug and a couple of slaps on the back. "Maggie, you look great for a mother of four," Perkins said.

Maggie smiled, gave him a hug and thanked him.

"Perkins," Jim started, "this is my right-hand man Pepie and his wife, Blue Sky. They're going to be Emma's godparents tomorrow."

"Here, sit down. Everyone want coffee?" Perkins said.

A lot of time was taken getting caught up on all the news.

"How are you feeling, Jim? How is that cough of yours?" Perkins asked.

"I'm having trouble, but Maggie and her medicine man keep me going. Someday soon I'd like to take a trip, maybe to Florida, see if that would help."

"You ready for dinner? We have stew or a big beef steak."

They all ordered the stew. They ate plenty of steak at the Judith.

The talk went on for another couple of hours. They arranged to have a party after the baptism at Perkins'.

The next day, after Maggie and Blue Sky came back from shopping, Maggie was almost in tears. "Jim," she said, "you can't believe how we are treated out on the street and in the stores. One woman even told the store owner, 'If you allow dirty Indians in here, I'll shop somewhere else.' Jim, it was so bad."

"Maggie," Jim started in, "as long as we have these people coming from the East thinking they're better than all of us, we will have problems. Fort Benton is a white city."

"I want to leave as soon as possible tomorrow."

In the morning, the family of six walked down to the church. Once again, Maggie wore her funny hat, and Jim wore his suit. They were greeted at the door by Father Imoda. The Jesuits were still the only ones Jim trusted.

Jim introduced everyone to Father Imoda. The priest smiled. "This is a real western mix — whites, Mexicans and Indians, a true mix of the future."

"I'm pleased you think so, Father."

"Come in," the priest said.

The church was new, all wood and painted white. It had the baptismal bowl near the altar.

"Father, it's been many years since I've been in a church, and I've never been in a Catholic one."

"It's all right, Jim. God's house is for everyone, and this one is built strong and won't fall. Now, who are the godparents?"

Pepie and Blue Sky moved forward. "We are!"

"Good. This is what you are to read, and I will help you answer. Any questions?"

The baptism took about twenty minutes, and Emma slept right through it.

"Father," Jim said. "We're having a party over at Perkins' restaurant. We want you to come over. Perkins has some watered-down rock gut that he'll try to get rid of on us."

"Jim, I would like to come over, but I can only stay until five o'clock. I have confession here at church."

The party was a lot of fun. But Jim and Maggie and the children were happy to get back in the wagon the next day for the Judith. The trip back was uneventful, but they all noticed how much more of the land was being plowed and planted in wheat.

All that winter, Jim talked to Maggie about taking the children and going to Florida for a year. Things at the Judith would run themselves and, if they took the last boat downriver in the fall of 1881, it would give them almost a year to get ready. Maggie was worried; she had never been so far from home. But Jim kept insisting that he wanted to try Florida for his cough. She finally agreed.

The one thing Maggie wanted to do before the trip was spend a little time with her family so the children could learn some of the ways of her people.

It was a gift that the Judith had another mild winter,

which meant early boats and a good crop of calves. That was a noise Jim could never forget, when the cattle were rounded up and the cows separated from their calves. All those cows hanging around the corrals, bellowing for their young. Finally when they got hungry they would leave, but you could still hear them off in the distance. The male calves were castrated, branded, held for a couple of weeks then turned out to pasture. This happened in early spring. The steers were separated for sale.

And the dock was repaired and readied for the boats as they came upriver. The total tonnage for Fort Benton and places below reached 17,420 tons, which was the most ever.

On April 2, Matt Duncan, one of Jim's herders, was killed at the Judith by hostile Indians. Jim sent word to Sheriff Healy in Fort Benton, and also to the Army. The death of Matt Duncan put fear in many of Jim's ranch hands. But he wasn't going to let it stop his plans for that trip to Florida.

In June, Maggie and Blue Sky took all the children to the Gros Ventre camp on up on the Milk River. By the end of July, Jim was ready to join them, and set out for the Gros Ventre summer camp. It took him about four days to reach it. When he arrived, he could see that many of the tipis looked tattered, since the Gros Ventres were finding fewer buffalo.

He could see the lodge of his father-in-law. It was in the best shape, since he had Maggie to help him that summer. Maggie and the children ran out to greet Jim and were quick to pull him into the tipi. "Welcome, Jim, to my lodge. It is always good to see you," Horse Capture said.

"It is always good to see you, Chief, and to see you in such good health." The women had prepared a big meal of buffalo meat for Jim. The children seemed happy, running in and out of the tipi.

"How are things here, really?" Jim asked.

Capture looked at Jim with regret. "We are to share our reservation with our enemy, the Nakota people, or as the whites call them, the Assiniboines."

Jim told Capture that most of the other tribes were already on reservations or had escaped to Canada, but he didn't think it would be any better up there.

Over the summer Maggie had let the children just be Indian children. She felt that every game they played prepared them for adult roles. The boys had miniature bows and were allowed to hunt small game. Maggie had made Mary and Emma dolls and toy tipis. She said that they also played in all the boys' games.

Jim was tired, and they all settled down for the night. Maggie had to wake her father so he could leave his seat and lie down under his buffalo robe. Jim was amazed that the tipi contained four adults and seven children and was not crowded: himself, Maggie, their four children, Blue Sky and her three children.

They next day Jim was to have a sweat with the medicine man. Maggie felt that he could help Jim's cough as he had in the past. The medicine man was pleased to see Jim and had the sweat lodge ready. This medicine men had his own specialty and knew his herbs, which he would use both externally and internally to combat sickness. The medicine man was worried about Jim's lungs.

After the sweat Jim went down to the river to bathe. He was so tired; all his energy had been drained. He went into his lodge and slept all afternoon. When he awoke, Maggie had dinner ready, but he was still so tired it was hard to stay awake. As soon as he finished dinner, Jim went back to bed and slept all night.

He woke early and took Lee and William hunting. They

shot a young antelope and brought it back to camp, pleasing Maggie greatly.

Jim spent a week at the camp, then wanted to head back to the Judith. Plans were made to leave the next morning. It was hard on Maggie to leave. She felt that she would not see her father again. There were many hugs and tears from the children as they said goodbye to their grandfather.

The trip back took four days. Jim drove the wagon and had his horse tied behind. Lee was sitting next to Jim. "Dad, can we go see your mother and father someday?"

"Lee," Jim said, "My parents died, back in Indiana. We had a trading post and farm. But that's a long, long time ago."

They would have a good trip to Florida. It would be their first trip together as a family.

How Jim hated to see this great country change. Montana Territory was so rough and beautiful. It was the country of the "short grass." The blazing summer sun turned it brown after a brief spring. The short grass could be cut and stacked for feed for the long winter, but when it stayed on the ground it provided feed for the animals the whole year around.

The best hay was wild bluestem hay. Jim could cut two hayrack loads in one day, as much as six or seven tons a week. But in Montana, the hay was only necessary for emergencies. Livestock could graze well into December. After that, the livestock could continue to graze, getting water from eating the snow.

The cattlemen loved the grass which the plow was destroying.

Still, the Army reported that in 1880, central Montana was mostly uninhabited. Patches of buffalo still darkened the rolling plains. And there were deer, antelope, elk, wolves and coyotes everywhere.

By now, in the whole Territory of Montana, there were 250,000 head of cattle.

Changes were coming to Montana.

When the family returned to the Judith, all energy went into preparing for the trip to Florida.

CHAPTER THIRTEEN

The Trip To Florida

ON SEPTEMBER 7, 1881, the Big Horn arrived at the Judith. She was eight days early but would stay docked until the 15th. Jim had reserved a cabin with beds for the whole family. The day before they boarded the boat, Jim met with all his men to smooth out any last-minute problems. Cap said, "Jim, we'll miss you, but the Judith will be here when you come back. Just have a good trip and don't worry."

Jim, Maggie and the four children boarded the Big Horn the evening of the 14th and had a buffalo dinner with the Captain. The Captain told Jim that he ate so much buffalo on his trips up the Missouri that he felt he was getting a hump. Jim said, "Eat them now. At the rate they're killing them, it won't be long before they're all gone."

"There is no way anyone could kill all those buffalo around here," the captain came back.

"Just wait," Jim said.

Jim and Maggie woke early to watch the boat leave the Judith. Blue Sky, Pepie and their children were on the dock along with Cap, Little John and Jim, and about half of the men. Everyone waved and shouted goodbyes as the boat pulled out of the Judith River and into the current of the Missouri. It wasn't long before the post was out of sight.

"Well, Maggie, it's too late for you to change your mind."

Jim found himself a nice place on the bow of the ship, where he could watch their movement down the Missouri.

Later, when the children woke, Jim and Maggie tied thin ropes around their waists. Lee and William protested that they were too old for ropes and could swim. Jim told them not in the Missouri. The boys ran up and down the deck a hundred times that first morning.

In the afternoon they passed the Crow River. It was interesting how many memories the river brought back to Jim. The boat parked about twenty miles below the Crow for the night. They were fed an early dinner and all were in bed early. Again the next day, Jim was up early, had his coffee and watched them prepare the boat for the second day's trip. The boats still traveled from first light to last.

Around noon on the second day, the river made a sharp bend south. Jim gathered Maggie and the kids on deck. "We're coming to the Musselshell, or Shell River. This is where we had one of our trading posts, but now it's under water," Jim announced.

On the third night they stopped at old Fort Peck at the Milk River. This also was the site of one of Jim's old trading posts. Jim remembered the five men who had lived there: the Boss, a Frenchman known as Joe Bushway — a very able fellow. John Fattig, the burly giant with a black beard and whose voice roared. Fattig's partner Davis. Then there were the twins, Jim and Tim McGinnis. Jim wondered what had happened to all those people.

The boat took on cedar wood at the Milk River. Back when

Jim sold wood to the boats, he made five to six dollars a cord for cottonwood and eight to twenty dollars for cedar. He wondered what the boats had to pay now. He had heard they were paying thirteen dollars a cord for cottonwood in Fort Benton, so cedar must be at a premium.

Jim walked off the boat, but the Fort Peck he remembered was gone. Now it was just a woodhawks' stockade with a few old buildings. From Fort Peck, going east through Montana Territory, it was bleak, hot and dry.

A couple of miles before they hit the Yellowstone they passed beneath the palisades of Fort Union, where the American Fur Company was established. At the junction of the Missouri and the Yellowstone had once stood the Fort Union trading post, which was taken apart to build Fort Buford. Where the Yellowstone River, known to the Indians as "Elk River," entered the Missouri, the river became wider and movement for the boat easier.

From here they moved into the fantastic Pinnacles of the Dakota Badlands. Passing old Fort Berthold, they could see Indian burial grounds where hundreds of weather-beaten platforms on slender poles held Indian mummies.

They passed through the Mandans' village. Here the cone-shaped huts were built of Missouri River mud. Two days later they arrived at the City of Bismarck. This was the kick-off point for people going into the Montana Territory and was as far as the railroad had come west.

As the Wells family went south after Bismarck, they passed one fort after another: Fort Yates, Fort Pierre, Fort Thompson. They finally arrived at Chamberlain, which was the former Fort Kiowa. It took them almost five weeks to reach St. Louis. Here the boat stopped for two days to re-supply before the final leg of the trip to New Orleans. This would take another two weeks.

The section from St. Louis on was an easy trip. St. Louis was still the gateway to the West and especially to California. It was a wild city with little law. Jim and Maggie thought it best if they stayed on the boat with the children.

The boat arrived in New Orleans the first of November. Jim and the family planned to stay there for a week before taking a stage to Florida. New Orleans sat on a great bend of the Mississippi, about a hundred and ten miles upriver from the Gulf. The city was protected by levees. There were more boats of all kinds than Jim had ever seen in his life, even when he was in San Francisco. The weather was cool. Jim and Maggie were amazed at the courtesy and respect with which they were treated. The one thing they noticed was that their clothes were unusual for New Orleans; they would go shopping the next day.

They found a hotel in the center of the city. The hotel gave them a suite that had two bedrooms and a sitting room, and they would put in extra beds for the children.

In New Orleans lived many mixed bloods who had wealth. French Louisiana had been ceded to Spain in 1762, then back to France before the United States purchased it in 1803. So there were a lot of French-Black mixes who were called French-Creole. But all were equal, which gave the whole city a good feeling.

That feeling was everywhere when they went shopping for store-bought clothes. Gone were the stupid stares and ugly looks which Maggie had to see in Fort Benton. Jim looked in a mirror. "I sure look funny, but you, Maggie, are beautiful. The only thing I won't give up is my six-shooter. It's part of my dress."

The four days were full for the Wells family: the opera, plays, and new kinds of food. The children were good and stood with their mouths open, taking it all in. It was hard for them to leave New Orleans, but Jim and Maggie promised that they would come back and stay longer.

It was a six-day journey to Jacksonville, Florida. The stage made overnight stops along the way, from Mobile to Tallahassee and on to Jacksonville, which made it easier. Jim was having trouble with his cough and was short of breath. He decided to see a doctor right away when they arrived. In Jacksonville they planned to stay a couple of days, buy a carriage and a few good horses. Then their travels in Florida would begin.

Jacksonville, to Jim's surprise, was ten miles inland and not on the Atlantic Ocean. But it was full of history for them to see. The harbor reminded Jim of San Francisco, a port with land all around.

They settled at a hotel and Jim asked the owners if they could recommend a doctor. They gave him the name of Dr. Matthew Johnson. Jim excused himself from the family and went to make an appointment right away. He was feeling weak and wanted to know his prognosis as soon as possible.

Jim found the doctor's office. He told the secretary that he was staying at the Jacksonville Hotel and that they had given him Dr. Johnson's name. She gave him a form to fill out:

NAME: James Wells
RESIDENCE: Montana
AGE: 46
PROBLEM: Bad cough, short of breath
PAYMENT: Cash

After he had filled it out, she said, "The doctor can see you in about five minutes. Is that all right?"

"Thank you. I'll wait." Jim sat down.

Shortly, Jim was taken into a small room with a wooden table and chair and a medicine cabinet. "Take off your clothes; the doctor will be right in."

Jim smiled and took off his pants and shirt but left on his long johns. After a few minutes the doctor came in. He was short and fat, with a moustache, goatee and the funniest glasses Jim had ever seen.

"Mr. Wells, I'm Doctor Johnson."

"Pleased to meet you. I'm Jim Wells from Montana."

"Please, Mr. Wells, take off the long johns so I can give you a complete exam.

"All right," Jim said.

The doctor looked Jim over for a moment.

"Mr. Wells, you been in the war? You have a lot of scars."

"No, doctor, just life in Montana."

The doctor adjusted the side of the funny glasses, making a second glass. He looked into Jim's eyes, nose, ears and throat. He put a cup on Jim's chest that had tubes connected to his ears. "Mr. Wells, will you please take some deep breaths for me?"

Jim tried to. He started coughing.

"Mr. Wells, how long have you had this cough and trouble breathing?"

"Well, the cough I've had for years. Only been short of breath the last year."

"Mr. Wells, you have consumption, and it is bad. You know what consumption is? It's a wasting disease. It's serious."

Jim looked at the doctor. "I came to Florida to help the cough. What do you think?"

"Mr. Wells, I think it will help, but to be honest, I think it's too late. You are a very sick man. How long are you going to be in Florida?"

"We plan to be here until July of this year."

"Good," the doctor said. "You should have another check-up before you go back to Montana. I'll give you something for that cough."

"Doctor, how much more time do I have?" Jim said.

"Mr. Wells, I would give a man in your condition five years at the most."

"Even if he's as tough as me?"

"Mr. Wells, it's destroying your lungs. Good luck, and I'm sorry the news isn't better. Here is your cough medicine — you can get refills anywhere."

"Thank you, Doctor, for seeing me." Jim shook his hand.

Jim dressed and went out to the front desk. The woman looked at him and said, "That will be two dollars fifty cents, plus fifty cents for the medicine. Doctor Johnson said to tell you you are always welcome."

Jim paid and said, "Thank you for your help."

He didn't go right back to the hotel. He took a long walk so he could think. After awhile he found a place that sold carriages and horses. He went in and, being a good horse trader, felt he made a good bargain on a complete rig, big enough for his whole family. He drove his new rig back to the hotel and gave it to the boy at the door. "You take good care of these horses," he said.

"Yes sir," the boy came back.

Jim decided not to tell Maggie. Maybe he would get better.

"Maggie, get the kids ready. I bought us a rig."

"Jim," she asked, "what did the doctor say?"

"He said that Florida would be good for me and gave me some cough medicine. So, Maggie, this trip is the right thing for us."

They took a ride out to the northeast side of Jacksonville to see Yellow Bluff Fort, which sat on a cliff and could stop all shipping coming into the port. Jim was amazed at the strong brick fort, after seeing those wood stockades they built up in Montana. "This fort," he told Maggie, "was built to last forever, not just a couple of seasons like ours."

From the fort they went out to the Kingsley Plantation, which had survived the Civil War. On it was a beautiful house, with the most beautiful gardens and grounds.

"Maggie, this give you some ideas for a new home?" Jim joked.

"Jim, what would you do with all this room, and how would you heat the place?"

"Maggie, that's why it's in Florida where it's warm and you don't have to worry about heat."

After a few days in Jacksonville they were ready to move on. Maggie had taken the family out to buy swimwear for when they at last saw the Atlantic Ocean.

And early that afternoon they saw it. Maggie and the boys just stood there, unable to believe any water could be that big. "Get those shoes off and walk in!" Jim yelled.

It wasn't long before they were all wet. "The water is salty!" Lee called out.

Jim laughed. "Yes, it's salty and drink too much, it'll come right back up."

They found a place to spend the night on the coast, and the children were out in the water until the sun went down. The first sunset Jim saw was a shock. In San Francisco the sun went down over the water, and here it went down over the land. It was also a strange sight when the sun came up over the water in the morning.

"Maggie, this is your trip, so we stay where you want as long as you want."

They started down the coast, amazed by the trees full of beautiful oranges. A basket of oranges was one of their first purchases. Maggie and the children had never eaten them.

"Jim, these are the juiciest fruits I have ever seen!"

By Christmas they had been traveling slowly down the coast for over a month, enjoying every day of it. The children were so brown they could pass for full-blood Indians.

They found a village near Fort Pierce and rented a house for a couple of weeks so they could have Christmas and New

Year's in one place. Jim was able to buy a tree and Maggie decorated it with berries and things the children made. She went into town and was able to buy clothes and toys and dolls. The children were happy with their presents. It was one of the few times Santa Claus had brought store-bought toys to them. It was a good Christmas, but Jim and Maggie missed all their friends at the Judith.

Jim was feeling good. He coughed less and felt the sun was curing him.

New Year's was wild at the Fort. A lot of guns and cannons were fired, and the children were allowed to stay up as the year 1882 was, as Jim said, "shot in."

It took them another month to reach the Florida Keys and the Mangrove Swamp. Jim found a small home which they rented for the month of February. Jim and the family took many trips out to the Everglades and the swamps. They saw alligators which made Maggie scream.

They left the east coast of Florida the first week in March and crossed the Everglades toward Fort Myers. It was a hundred-and-fifty mile trip. On the west coast they found the Gulf of Mexico calm and warm.

Jim, being the businessman he was, was thinking of buying a freight wagon, loading it with oranges packed in straw and taking them back to Fort Benton. He might be able to pay for this whole trip.

The next three months were spent traveling up the west coast of Florida, through Sarasota where Jim and Maggie went to the horse races. After a day at the tracks, Jim told Maggie, "I sure thought I knew my horses. We didn't win one race."

"Jim, the horses you know are a different kind."

It was true. These horses were small and skinny. Wouldn't get much work out of them. A bull would throw one clear across Montana.

Next was Tampa, and on up the coast. The trip ended back
at Tallahassee.

In Tallahassee, Jim spent a week buying a freight wagon
with a team while selling his carriage and team for what he
had paid. The freight wagon was big and required four horses.

The next thing to do was buy oranges, oranges that were a
little green and would last into the fall. Jim was in his glory,
buying and trading. By the end of the week he had a freighter
loaded with straw and packed with fruit.

It was the middle of June — that gave them five weeks to
get to St. Louis, where they would board the Rosebud back to
the Judith. The trip was about seven hundred miles: they would
drive about twenty miles a day.

It took a week to make it to Montgomery. Here Jim checked
the wagon over. Everything looked good. Then two more weeks
to get to Nashville. It was an easy trip, with flat or rolling
hills. Jim was pleased at how the wagon, the team and his
family were holding up. This kind of traveling was very
different from what Jim had experienced in the west. Every
night they were able to find an inn or hotel, as there were many
villages and towns along the way.

The last part of the trip, from Nashville to St. Louis, was
uneventful and they found they were a couple of days ahead of
schedule. In St. Louis they found a nice hotel near the
waterfront, and Jim turned Maggie loose to do her last shopping
for herself and for friends back at the Judith.

Jim went down to the dock and arranged for his freight to be
stored and made ready for the Rosebud, which would be
leaving on August 15 from St. Louis.

After he stored his oranges, Jim took the wagon and horses
down to the stockyard. He was looking for someone wanting to
go west. He put the horses in a stable and put the word out that
they were for sale.

Within two days, a big Dutchman contacted Jim. He gave Jim the price he had paid for the freighter and team. The Dutchman didn't even bargain. He handed Jim the money and asked for a "Bill of Sale" for his purchase. They walked over to the stable and Jim introduced the Dutchman as the new owner of his team and wagon to the stable owner.

"You got a good team and wagon, mister," the stable man said.

The Dutchman nodded his head yes and told the stable man he would pick them up the next day. Jim paid for his part of the care. "Mister, what you bringing up in that big wagon?" the stable man asked.

"Oranges," Jim said, as he walked off.

He went back to the hotel. "Maggie, I sold the wagon and team. We didn't lose a dollar. Now I'm sure I can make money on those oranges. Just think — the first oranges in Montana Territory."

"Jim, you are a good trader. I'm proud of you."

The departure date was still August 15, so they moved on board on August 14. Jim asked that his freight be stored on a cool part of the boat, and he was on site to watch the loading. The captain asked Jim what was so special about his freight. Jim looked at him with a smile and said, "Oranges."

The captain looked surprised and said, "Oranges — that's a first for me."

The Rosebud pulled into the river early on the morning of August 15 for the final upriver trip of the season.

Maggie had done one thing in St. Louis: she had a picture of herself and Jim taken (the children would not sit still), so she could remember Jim in his store-bought clothes. The first day out, Jim packed away those clothes and put his buckskins back on.

Jim found his spot again on the bow of the ship so he could

watch the landmarks pass as the days went on. Since they left
Florida, Jim's cough had returned, but he had stocked up on his
medicine in St. Louis. The water was up and the boat was
moving at a good speed, but it would still take another five
weeks. Jim was now anxious to get home, as were Maggie and
the children.

Jim wondered what had happened to the famous Chocteau
family, who had owned posts all the way up the river from St.
Louis to Fort Benton. But they had backed the Confederacy, so
when the war ended they lost their licenses, and were forced to
sell to the Northwest Fur Company of Hubble and Hawley.
Also the Army moved into some of their trading posts.

It took more wood to push the steamboat upstream than
down: thirty to thirty-five cords for every twenty-four hours of
steaming. The boats couldn't carry all that wood so woodhawks
were all along the river. Everyday they heard the cry, "Wood-
up!"

Jim still saw a lot of Mackinaws, and while they traveled
fast downstream, loaded in the middle with furs and rowed by
up to four men, they usually broke apart by the end of the
journey or were hit by steamboats.

As the days passed, Jim and his family came again upon
the village of the Mandans. Some sat on top of their domed
huts wrapped in buffalo robes, watching the boat steam by.

Back through the Dakota Badlands to the place where the
Yellowstone and the Missouri came together. It was interesting
how the Missouri narrowed. Then the Milk River and the
Musselshell. They were getting close to the Judith.

The steamboat arrived on schedule at the Judith the
evening of September 20, 1882. There was a large group to meet
the boat, all there to welcome the Wells family back. Jim felt
great putting his feet back on the earth of the Judith. They
were home.

The Rosebud unloaded its one hundred fifty tons of cargo, including Jim's oranges.

Their house had been cleaned and painted, and wildflowers were in bouquets in the windows. Blue Sky looked at Maggie. "You look good. But are you going to have another baby?"

"Yes," Maggie answered, "and it will be here by Christmas."

Jim got up early the next morning and gave everyone a bag of oranges. He packed a wagon for Helena with two-thirds of the fruit, and a wagon for Fort Benton with the rest. The oranges were making the last part of their trip.

The Judith was in good condition and was already in preparation for winter. They had had only two boats that summer, the Emily on June 7 with two hundred tons, and the Rosebud with its one hundred fifty tons. But the cattle business and trading post were doing well.

Jim was able to sell all his oranges in Helena to hotels for $1 each, and in Fort Benton for $.75 each. His profit was very good. He paid for his whole trip and had money left over. He would be known as "Orange Jim," the man who brought the first oranges to Montana.

A fifth child was born to Jim and Maggie on December 2, 1882. He was named James after his father.

Jim had a hard winter. His cough and breathing condition were worsening.

Jim and Maggie also received word that their friend Father Giorda had died of a heart ailment at Sacred Heart Mission on August 4, 1882.

Now a boys' school would be opened in the spring at St. Peter's Mission, which was one day's journey from Helena. Jim and Maggie talked about sending Lee and William to St. Peter's

for school, so they made a trip to St. Peter's to talk to the
superior, Father Joseph Damiani. The school occupied a couple
of small cabins, one for living and the other for class. They had
a lay teacher to help the Jesuits: Louis Riel. Riel caused the
Jesuits some concern with his opinions on religion and politics,
but was a good teacher.

Jim and Maggie liked the situation at St. Peter's and
arranged to have Lee and William begin as students there.

Jim also learned that they were trying to open a girls'
school at St. Peter's. For this, Bishop Brondel had offered
Mother Amadeus a farm adjoining the mission, two wagons
with horses, and two milk cows, two hundred dollars worth of
provisions such as meat, flour, beans or whatever they needed.
Not only that but the Jesuits would spend $200 on repairs on the
old house which would be rented to the sisters for five dollars a
year (it would accommodate twenty girls or more); and last, if
instead of three sisters there could be four, one of the sisters
could teach the boys and get two hundred dollars a year from
the Jesuits.

All this helped, and the Ursuline sisters promised a school
by the summer of 1884 for girls. They would provide a fourth
sister to teach the boys. Jim wanted Mary to go to school at St.
Peter's as soon as the girls' school was open.

In the summer of 1883, the river boat companies had their
first scare with the completion of the Northern Pacific
Railroad to Helena on June 12, 1883 and the Canadian Pacific to
Calgary. The Northern Pacific was a blow to the Judith since
Helena had been their biggest source of customers. That summer
the Judith had only one boat, the Rosebud, with 150 tons of
freight. But what helped the Judith was the increased demand
for Montana beef.

Jim still believed that beef was the future of Montana.
That summer, Jim saw very few buffalo skins for shipping. The

Army sent out a report stating that by the fall of 1883 there would not be one buffalo remaining on the range; antelope, elk and deer were now scarce; and cattle would be up to 600,000 head.

As the buffalo were going, the Indians were also going. In 1835, the Gros Ventres numbered 10,000; now they and the Assiniboines combined were less than 2,000. The government was still trying to put them on a reservation. Jim and Maggie had a friend, Father Frederick Eberschweiler, who was the same age as Jim. He had come from St. Peter's to help the Indians receive their fair share, or at least get some land that wasn't desolate so they would not be reduced to beggary.

On his way to work with the Gros Ventres, Father Eberschweiler stopped at the Judith and baptized Jim and Maggie's new baby, James. Father Eberschweiler told Jim and Maggie how well Lee and William were doing in school. They would be home at the end of the summer for two weeks before the fall term started. He was pleased by the education they had received from Maggie and the teacher at the Judith.

The United States post office came to Jim and asked him to be postmaster for the Judith area.

Every year had its stories. Fort Benton had always run into fuel shortages, so the Benton Boom and Lumber Company would cut and float logs down the Missouri from timbered areas upriver. The boom would guide the logs into a bywater which was constructed to steer the timber into a retrieval area. But the river was too wide and fast-moving, and the affair flopped. Jim got many of the logs at the Judith.

Building at Fort Benton had slowed due to the railroad scare. Perkins told Jim, "Look at Peter MacDoland of the Pacific Hotel Saloon. He's lowered his drinks to one bit." But Jim knew that the beef in the markets, such as Porterhouse and sirloin steak, was a costly twenty-five cents a pound.

And T.C. Power told Jim he had one of his best years ever.

The River Press of January 2, 1883 included a map which showed the proposed route of the railroad. It would come across the Dakota and Montana plains by the St. Paul, Minneapolis & Manitoba Railroad. It would join the Canadian Pacific coming from the Medicine Hat area, just above Fort Benton. Then up from Billings and skirting the west side of the high woods was the Benton branch of the Northern Pacific. Just as Jim thought, the railroad was coming.

One night, Jim told Maggie he wanted to sell the Judith and retire to Fort Benton. He felt his health was going and he wanted the family settled before anything happened to him. Maggie held back tears but understood. Then Jim held a meeting with his men. He felt that the Judith was established and would go on, so their jobs would be safe. He would put Mary at St. Peter's in the summer and start looking for a buyer. So Jim sent word to Mr. Power, asking if he knew anyone who wanted to buy his interest.

In June he was contacted by Mr. Norris, who would buy out his interest, continue to run the ranch and keep the trading post going. A price was agreed upon and the papers signed and transferred on July 1, 1884.

Lee, William and Mary were now at St. Peter's. Jim let it be known that the children were not to be treated as half-breeds, and if they were he would pull them out of the school.

Jim and Maggie located a house in Fort Benton, and the purchase was put into the transaction of the sale of the Judith. Jim wanted all business to go through the First National Bank because it was locally owned and backed by Conrads of Baker, the Powers, Ed Maclay of Murphy, Neel and Scott Wetzel, and Sam Hauser from Helena.

The house was near old Fort Benton and had four bedrooms

and a porch that ran all the way around the house. It had a garden and a shed for the horse and carriage. "I had half of Montana," Jim told Maggie, "and now I only have one house."

"Jim, here you can get care. You must get better, for me and the children."

"Maggie, I think this consumption is going to win."

"Don't say that. Will you do me one favor, please? Just one."

"Maggie, I'd do anything for you."

"Many years ago you went to the sacred water in the Gros Ventre Mountains. I want you to go again, please."

"Maggie, that's three hundred miles away and way down in Wyoming."

"Jim, just for me."

"I will, Maggie, as soon as I get all my business out of the way."

"Jim, remember that the healing water only flows in the summer."

At the bank, Jim, T.C. Power and the bank president sat down together in the president's office. Jim made a will with T.C. Power and his brother John as the executors. Maggie couldn't hold property since she was an Indian, and the children were all too young — Lee, the oldest, was only thirteen.

"Jim, I have all the papers for you to sign."

"Power," Jim said, "you will have full power over all my money. It is Maggie's, but by law an Indian can't own property, so you must take care of Maggie and the children. I want Maggie to stay in that house if that is what she wants, and I want my children to receive their education. I want them to live as well as they live now. As you know, I am wealthy, and it is all their money. If you are not honest with them, may God, if there is one, damn your soul."

"Jim," Power responded, "you and I have always been fair partners, isn't that true?"

"Yes, but sometimes money makes a man change."

"Well, in any case, Jim, you will live a long life."

"No, T.C., I think this is my last year. The lungs are about gone."

The men signed three copies and each party kept a copy. Then they all shook hands. Jim came home mad.

"Maggie, it isn't right that you can't control our money, but here are the papers, with Mr. Power responsible. Please put them in a safe place."

By mid-July, Jim had everything in order. Maggie was settled into their new home and had a garden growing.

"Maggie, I think you put that garden in too late for results."

"I know, Jim, but it looks good."

"Maggie, I'm going to make that trip to the Gros Ventre Mountains. Figure I can be back in two weeks."

"Thank you, Jim."

Jim would leave the next morning and would go as far as St. Peter's so he could see his children.

He was up early. Maggie had everything ready. He saddled his horse and gave Maggie a big hug and kiss. "Maggie, I do love you."

"Jim, be careful. I love you and will pray for you."

That first day's trip, about forty-five miles, was a long push and Jim didn't get to St. Peter's until late. He was greeted by Father Damiani, who called Lee and William. Jim couldn't see Mary until morning, as the girls were already in bed.

Jim was fed and given a bed for the night. Lee and William were given permission to stay up late to talk to their father. It felt so good for Jim to see his boys. They were all over him, telling him about school, asking questions about their parents' new life in Fort Benton. Whenever he coughed, he saw how worried they looked. In the morning Jim had breakfast with Mary. She looked so little to be away at school. He gave his children a hug as they went off to class. He thanked the priests and was on his way.

Jim decided to ride cross-country. He felt that if he followed the Smith River it would be the fastest way. Two days later he was in Bozeman. He found a hotel room, cleaned up, had a good meal and was on the trail early, still heading south. He went right through Yellowstone, now a National Park. His next stop was Jackson. From Jackson it was a day-and-a-half ride into the Salt River Range and the healing springs.

Jim spent two days camping and bathing in the spring. It was a wonder. He would sit in a dry river bed, then hear thunder from the mountain and out would come a torrent of ice-cold water. It was a massive flow. Then it would dry up, to flow again fifteen minutes later. This would go on day and night, but it was known to stop in August, only to start flowing again in May. The Gros Ventres felt that there was much power there.

When Jim arrived home he was very tired and weak and all the healing that had occurred at the springs had worn off. "Maggie, I think my time for taking trips is about over."

Maggie was worried. His cough was worse and he didn't want to see the doctor. She realized that Jim had learned her ways — he knew his fate. She could only be at his side now.

Jim's new routine was to get up early, walk down to Perkins' for coffee, make the rounds of the docks, and come home for a noon meal with Maggie.

By the first of November, he was very weak. "Maggie, I must talk to you. I don't think I will last until spring," Jim said.

Maggie started to cry.

"No, Maggie, don't cry," Jim said. "This is what I want. We'll bring the children home at Christmas and they'll stay home. I want them with me."

Maggie agreed.

"When I die, get Perkins to take me out along the Missouri and bury me. Family and Perkins only — no graveyard, you understand."

Maggie said, "Yes."

"I want us to have the best Christmas, Maggie. Buy whatever you want."

The children would be home two weeks before Christmas and wouldn't go back until the middle of January. Jim and Maggie planned to have the tree up and decorated before the children arrived. They could still string berries and popcorn but Maggie would get some store-bought decorations. They also wanted to get presents, and have them hidden for the children to find. Jim's energy was going fast, but he was enjoying this Christmas preparation.

The children arrived home on December 6 by stage from Helena. Jim couldn't make the trip to pick them up. But they were very happy to be home and the talk went on and on into the night.

The next morning, Jim took Lee and William down to Perkins' with him to have coffee.

"You are good-looking boys. How old are you now?" Perkins asked.

Lee looked at him and said, "I'm thirteen, sir."

William piped up, "I'm ten, sir."

"Perkins, put a lot of milk in their coffee, say about half and half."

"Jim, you don't look so good. How are you feeling?"

"Perkins, you may be helping Maggie sooner than I thought."

"Jim, you shouldn't talk like that."

"I get less and less air every day. But Perkins, you're still on for Christmas Eve at our house."

The next two weeks were spent preparing for Christmas. They all baked bread, cookies, and pies and shopped for everything they wanted. To Jim it was wonderful to have his family around him.

Christmas Eve dinner with the Perkins' was great. The food just kept coming. After dinner, Jim told the children to get to bed so Santa Claus could come.

Perkins and Jim sat by the fire and had a drink while Molly and Maggie were in the kitchen.

Perkins said, "Jim, you're not doing good at all."

"No, and I want you to promise that Maggie is taken care of. I know you can't do much, but keep an eye out."

"I promise, Jim."

Christmas morning was all for the children. They received everything they wanted, from dolls to clothes to spending money. The excitement was something. The children spent the day playing indoors and out. Lee and William had new sleighs and stayed outside until they couldn't stand the cold anymore.

"This is a Christmas the children and I will always remember," Maggie told Jim.

By mid-January 1885, when the children were to return to St. Peter's, Jim was very sick and, as he had planned, they stayed home.

Maggie called the doctor to look at Jim. "Jim, you are real sick," the doctor told him.

"I know it, Doctor. It's consumption. The doctor in Florida told me that my lungs were wasting. He gave me no hope."

"Jim, he was right. Your lungs are filling."

"Please let me talk to Maggie."

"Jim, if you need anything, send someone to my office."

Maggie came in. "What did the doctor tell you?"

"Maggie, I don't have much more time. You know how much I love you. You have been my life. But please don't cry."

Jim went into a coma on February 1, 1885.

On February 11, Jim Wells died with his family around him.

Perkins came right away. He hugged Maggie and went into the bedroom. After he closed the door, Maggie could hear him crying, "Jim, I just lost a good friend." A couple of minutes later, he opened the door and went out with Lee and William to bring in the coffin. Maggie cleaned and prepared Jim and put his suit on him. They placed Jim in the coffin. Lee nailed down the lid and the family carried him out to the wagon.

Word of Jim's death traveled fast through Fort Benton.

Perkins and the family took Jim about five miles down the Missouri River. They found a meadow that wasn't covered by snow, dug a grave, placed Jim in it, and covered the grave with rocks.

Maggie and the children said a prayer, then climbed back in the wagon to return to Fort Benton.

The River Press reported:

February 11, 1885
Death of James Wells

We are called upon to chronicle the death of one of our most esteemed and respected citizens. James Wells passed away this morning at 6 o'clock after a long and painful sickness. His death was not unexpected, as for the past year no hopes have been entertained for his recovery, although until within a short time he has been buoyed up with the idea that he would yet recover. For several weeks he has been confined to his house. The following particulars relative to Mr. Wells were furnished by Mr. John W. Power and others who have known him long and intimately.

He was born in Indiana about 1840 and was therefore about 45 years of age. When he came west we could not learn, but he was in California and Oregon in early years and came to Montana in 1865 or '66. In 1868 he had a trading post on Milk River, about twenty miles above old Fort Browning. The following year he entered into the employ of T.C. Power & Bro. and served them in different capacities until the winter of 1874, when they established a post on Milk River, near the Black Butte. Wells was placed in charge. The following fall he relieved T.J. Bogy at Fort Clagget, purchasing an interest in that post which he retained until last year, when he sold out to G.R. Norris. He was one of the noblest men that ever came to this country; generous to a fault; the soul of honor, and he will be sadly missed by his old-time friends and associates. He leaves a family of five children who are left amply provided for. Last year he made a will, appointing Mr. Power executor.

For about a week, Maggie and the children were not seen.

T.C. Power sent a message to Maggie saying he would be in the Fort Benton office the next day and must meet with her.

Power said, "Mrs. Wells, I'm so sorry about Jim, but my brother and I are executors and some decisions must be made."

"Mr. Power, I plan on staying in Fort Benton with my children."

"No, I'm afraid that won't work. Your children are half-breeds. The Gros Ventres are relocating themselves at Fort Belknap. You will go there with your youngest, James. The other four children will return to St. Peter's. Your house here will be sold."

"But my daughter Emma is too young."

"No, she's ready to start school."

Maggie already knew there was nothing she could do. "I see, Mr. Power, you are honoring Jim's wishes. How can you live with that?"

"I think I can live with that, Mrs. Wells. I'll give you a week. We'll give you a horse, a wagon and anything you want in the house." Power smiled at her. "It is best this way. Have the children ready to go back to school this week. I will send them."

To answer her children's questions, Maggie told them that she would visit very soon and that she would have a new home on the reservation and that they would come and see her there. Power, as promised, arranged for a wagon to come take the children back to St. Peter's later that week. They weren't ready when it arrived, and the children had to hurry out of the house with their arms full of toys and clothes, as much as they could carry away. Maggie grabbed all of her children in her arms and said goodbye.

The next day, a wagon came for Maggie and James. It was full of freight and she could only bring two bags. She left Fort Benton, never looking back.

EPILOGUE

AT FORT BELKNAP, Maggie was remarried to an Indian named Bulls Head. Women could not survive single on the reservation. She died in 1895.

Lee Roy Wells died at St. Peter's Mission in 1886. He was stacking hay and slid down the haystack. A pitchfork went into his stomach. He lived for four days.

William (Willy) went on to work for T.C. Power as a clerk in Fort Benton.

Mary worked summers taking care of T.C. Power's son before he became one of the first two U.S. Senators from Montana. On July 25, 1895, she married Joseph Gump, a foreman on the ranch at St. Peter's Mission.

Emma left St. Peter's with Mary. She also worked for T.C. Power.

James died on the reservation in 1897.

The archives in Helena for Senator T.C. Power contain many letters from the children begging for shoes and clothing, as well as requesting permission to visit their mother. The requests were denied. The children weren't to become "wild Indians" again.

As for James Wells' wealth?

Thomas C. Power died March 15, 1923, a very wealthy man.

BIBLIOGRAPHY

Banks, Eleanor. *Wandersong*. Caxton Printers, 1950.

Bruchac, Joseph. *The Native American Sweat Lodge*. Crossing Press, 1993.

Burlingame, Merrill G. *The Montana Frontier*. Big Sky Books, 1980.

Cody, William F. and Henry Inman. *The Great Salt Lake Trail*. Macmillan, 1898.

Cooper, John M. *The Gros Ventres of Montana: Part II, Religion and Ritual*. The Catholic University of America Press, 1975.

Costello, Gladys. "White Man Left His Name To A Mountain." *Phillips County News*, 1987.

"Death of James Wells." *The River Press*, Fort Benton, February 11, 1885.

Flannery, Regina. *The Gros Ventres of Montana: Part I, Social Life*. The Catholic University of America Press, 1975.

Fort Belknap Education Department. *Recollections of Fort Belknap's Past*. Fort Belknap Indian Community, 1982.

Fort Belknap Education Department. *War Stories of the White Clay People*. Fort Belknap Indian Community, 1982.

Fowler, Loretta. *Shared Symbols, Contested Meanings: Gros Ventre Culture and History, 1778-1984*. Cornell University Press, 1987.

Hardin, Floyd. *Campfires and Cowchips*. Floyd Hardin, 1972.

"Historic Building." *The River Press*, Fort Benton, December 13, 1989.

Horse Capture, George, editor. *The Seven Visions of Bull Lodge.* University of Nebraska Press, 1992.

Howard, Joseph Kinsey. *Montana: High, Wide, and Handsome.* University of Nebraska Press, 1983.

Jackson, W. Turrentine. *Wells Fargo Stagecoaching in Montana Territory.* Montana Historical Society Press, 1979.

Kroeber, A.L. *Ethnology of the Gros Ventres.* American Museum of Natural History, Anthropological Paper, vol. 1 pt. 4, 1908.

Lavender, David. *Let Me Be Free.* Harper Collins, 1992.

MacDonald, Henry. "A Pioneer." *The River Press*, Fort Benton, January 26, 1887.

Marshall, S.L.A. *Crimsoned Prairie: The Indian Wars.* Da Capo Press, 1972.

McBride, Genevieve. *The Bird Tail.* Vantage Press, 1974.

McHugh, Tom. *The Time of the Buffalo.* University of Nebraska Press, 1979.

Morgan, L.H. *The Indian Journal, 1859-1982.* University of Michigan Press, 1959.

Noyes, A.J. *In the Land of Chinook: The Story of Blaine County.* State Publishing Co., 1917.

Overholser, Joel. *Fort Benton: World's Innermost Port.* Joel Overholser, 1987.

Overholser, Joel. "James Wells Had Very Busy, Adventurous Life In Area." *The River Press*, Fort Benton, August 19, 1981.

Palladino, Laurence Benedict. *Indian & White In the Northwest: A History of Catholicity in Montana.* J. Murphy & Co., 1894.

Schoenberg, Wilfred. *Jesuits in Montana.* The Oregon Jesuit, 1960.

Toole, K. Ross. *Montana: An Uncommon Land.* University of Oklahoma Press, 1943.

Utley, Robert M. *The Indian Frontier of the American West, 1846-1890.* University of New Mexico Press, 1987.

Vogel, Virgil J. *American Indian Medicine.* University of Oklahoma Press, 1990.

Washburn, Wilcomb E. *Red Man's Land/White Man's Law.* University of Oklahoma Press, 1995.

White, Jon Manchip. *Everyday Life of the North American Indians.* Dorset Press, 1979.

Willard, John. *Adventure Trails in Montana.* State Publishing Co., 1964.

Winther, Oscar Osburn. *Via Western Express & Stagecoach.* Stanford University Press, 1945.

UNPUBLISHED SOURCES

Bureau of Indian Affairs, Fort Belknap Reservation:
    Office Files.
Montana Historical Society, Helena:
    Papers of T.C. Power.
National Archives, Records of the Bureau of Indian Affairs, Washington, D.C.:
    Central Files, Fort Belknap Agency.
    Indian Census Rolls, 1888-1911.